THE AUSTRALIAN Women's Weekly

100 FAMILY DINNERS

WE TEST ALL OUR RECIPES 3 TIMES

Our team of chefs at The Australian Women's Weekly Test Kitchen are working hard everyday to make sure each recipe you make at home works every time. The 'Test Kitchen', as we like to call it, is located right in the heart of Sydney, Australia.

D1513168

CONTENTS

· · · · · · · · · · · · · · · · · · · ·

beef & veal

steak bourguignon with celeriac potato mash

PREP + COOK TIME 40 MINUTES • SERVES 4

1 small celeriac (400g), chopped coarsely

2 medium potatoes (400g), chopped coarsely

¼ cup (60ml) milk

40g (1½ ounces) butter

cooking-oil spray

4 x 200g beef eye-fillet steaks

200g (6½ ounces) button mushrooms, halved

6 baby onions (150g), quartered

2 cloves garlic, crushed

½ cup (125ml) dry red wine

1 cup (250ml) beef stock

1 tablespoon tomato paste

1 tablespoon coarsely chopped fresh thyme

1 Boil, steam or microwave celeriac and potato, separately, until tender; drain. Mash in a medium bowl with milk and butter; cover to keep warm.

2 Meanwhile, spray a large frying pan with oil; heat over medium-high heat. Cook beef for 4 minutes each side or until browned and cooked as desired; remove from pan, cover to keep warm.

3 Cook mushrooms, onion and garlic in same pan until vegetables just soften. Add wine, stock and paste; simmer, uncovered, for 5 minutes or until sauce thickens slightly.

4 Serve beef with mash and bourguignon sauce; sprinkle with thyme.

serving suggestion Pan-fried baby carrots or steamed asparagus or broccoli.

beef and mushroom pot pies

PREP + COOK TIME 30 MINUTES • SERVES 4

1 sheet ready-rolled puff pastry

1 tablespoon olive oil

1 medium brown onion (150g), sliced thinly

1 clove garlic, crushed

250g (8 ounces) button mushrooms, quartered

500g (1 pound) beef rump steak, trimmed, sliced thinly

1 tablespoon plain (all-purpose) flour

½ cup (125ml) dry red wine

½ cup (125ml) beef stock

400g (12½ ounces) canned crushed tomatoes

2 tablespoons tomato paste

2 teaspoons fresh thyme leaves

1 Preheat oven to 200°C/400°F.

2 Cut pastry sheet into four squares.

3 Heat oil in a large frying pan over medium-high heat; cook onion and garlic, stirring, for 4 minutes or until onion softens. Add mushrooms; cook, stirring, for 2 minutes.

4 Toss beef with flour in a medium bowl, add to pan; cook, stirring, for 5 minutes or until beef is browned. Stir in wine, stock, tomatoes and paste; bring to the boil. Reduce heat to low; simmer, uncovered, for 10 minutes or until mixture thickens slightly. Stir in thyme.

5 Spoon beef mixture into 4 x 1-cup (250ml) square ramekins. Place pastry over each dish, securing with a little water; carefully cut a hole in the top of each pastry square. Bake for 15 minutes or until pastry is puffed and browned.

6 Serve pies with pea mash (see below), if you like.

serving suggestion We served our pies with a smashed pea & potato mash: combine a 475g (15 ounce) tub hot potato mash with 2 cups smashed steamed peas and 40g (1½ ounce) melted butter.

We used a shiraz-style wine in this recipe, you can use any red you have open.

cottage pie

2 teaspoons olive oil

1kg (2 pounds) minced (ground) lean beef

1 medium brown onion (150g), chopped finely

1 medium carrot (120g), sliced finely

1 trimmed celery stalk (100g), sliced finely

1 tablespoon chopped fresh thyme leaves

1 cup (250ml) beef stock

1 tablespoon worcestershire sauce

¼ cup (70g) tomato paste

400g (12½ ounces) canned diced tomatoes

½ cup (60g) frozen peas

2 tablespoons grated cheddar

POTATO TOPPING

6 medium potatoes (1.2kg), chopped coarsely

60g (2 ounces) butter

¼ cup (60ml) milk

1 Preheat oven to 180°C/350°F.
2 Heat oil in a large saucepan over high heat; cook beef and onion, stirring, for 5 minutes or until browned.
3 Add carrot, celery, thyme, stock, sauce, paste and tomatoes; simmer, uncovered, for 30 minutes or until carrots are tender. Add peas; cook for 10 minutes or until peas are tender and the liquid has thickened.
4 Meanwhile, to make potato topping, boil, steam or microwave potatoes until tender; drain. Mash potato with butter and milk.
5 Spoon beef mixture into a 10-cup (2.5-litre) ovenproof dish. Spread topping over beef mixture; sprinkle with cheese. Bake, uncovered, for 30 minutes or until pie is heated through and topping is golden. Serve sprinkled with extra thyme, if you like.

five-spice beef with almonds

PREP + COOK TIME 35 MINUTES • SERVES 4

750g (1½-pound) piece beef eye-fillet, sliced thinly

1 teaspoon garam masala

2 teaspoons chinese five-spice power

1 tablespoon peanut oil

1 medium carrot (120g), cut into long thin strips

1 large red capsicum (bell pepper) (350g), cut into long thin strips

2 cloves garlic, crushed

1 tablespoon finely grated fresh ginger

170g (5½ ounces) coarsely chopped choy sum

3 teaspoons sambal oelek

2 tablespoons oyster sauce

2 tablespoons mango chutney

2 tablespoons lime juice

2 tablespoons water

100g (3 ounces) snow peas, trimmed

1 cup (80g) bean sprouts

⅓ cup (55g) blanched almonds, toasted, chopped roughly

test kitchen notes

You can substitute the beef with chicken or pork. This recipe is not suitable to freeze.

1 Combine beef and spices in a large bowl; mix well.

2 Heat half the oil in a wok over high heat; stir-fry beef mixture, in batches, until beef is browned and tender, remove from wok.

3 Heat remaining oil in wok; add carrot, capsicum, garlic and ginger. Stir-fry for 2 minutes, then add choy sum, sambal, sauce, chutney, juice and the water; stir-fry for 4 minutes or until choy sum is tender.

4 Return beef to wok with snow peas and sprouts; stir-fry until heated through. Serve topped with nuts.

serving suggestion Steamed rice or rice noodles.

thai beef omelettes

PREP + COOK TIME 30 MINUTES • SERVES 4

2 tablespoons peanut oil

400g (14½ ounces) beef rump steak, sliced thinly

1 small brown onion (80g), sliced thinly

2 cloves garlic, crushed

2 tablespoons oyster sauce

8 eggs

1 teaspoon fish sauce

1 teaspoon soy sauce

100g (3 ounces) enoki mushrooms

½ cup each fresh mint and thai basil leaves

1 cup (80g) bean sprouts

1 long red chilli, seeded, cut into strips

1 Heat 2 teaspoons of the oil in a frying pan over high heat; stir-fry beef, in batches, until browned. Remove from wok.

2 Heat another 2 teaspoons of the oil in pan; stir-fry onion and garlic until fragrant. Return beef to pan with oyster sauce; stir-fry until hot. Remove from wok; cover to keep warm.

3 Whisk eggs with fish and soy sauces in a large jug. Heat 1 teaspoon of the oil in same pan; pour in a ¼ cup of the egg mixture, tilting the pan to make a 14cm (5½-inch) omelette, cook until almost set. Slide omelette onto a serving plate; cover to keep warm. Repeat to make a total of eight omelettes.

4 Fill omelettes with beef, mushrooms, herbs, sprouts and chilli.

Enoki mushrooms have clumps of long, spaghetti-like stems with tiny, snowy white caps. They are available from Asian food shops and supermarkets.

Test Kitchen NOTE

To make a 'net-style' omelette, place the egg mixture in a plastic ziptop bag. Snip a small hole in one corner and drizzle the mixture into a heated oiled wok.

spicy beef with noodles

PREP + COOK TIME 30 MINUTES • SERVES 4

500g (1 pound) udon noodles

2 tablespoons peanut oil

750g (1½ pounds) minced (ground) beef

1 small brown onion (80g), sliced thinly

2 cloves garlic, crushed

⅓ cup (95g) black bean sauce

2 medium carrots (240g), cut into matchsticks

1 bunch baby pak choy (400g), chopped coarsely

¼ cup (60ml) hoisin sauce

¼ cup (60ml) beef stock

2 tablespoons rice vinegar

2 tablespoons coarsely chopped fresh coriander leaves (cilantro)

1 Place noodles in a large heatproof bowl, cover with hot water; stand for 5 minutes, drain.
2 Heat oil in a wok over high heat; stir-fry beef, onion and garlic for 5 minutes or until beef is browned and almost cooked. Add black bean sauce; stir-fry until mixture is well browned.
3 Add noodles, carrot, pak choy, hoisin sauce, stock and vinegar; stir-fry for 3 minutes or until vegetables are just tender. Serve sprinkled with coriander.

test kitchen notes

Use a vegetable peeler to cut the carrot into ribbons. Swap the beef mince for pork and veal or chicken mince. This recipe is not suitable to freeze.

beef steak with capsicum relish

PREP + COOK TIME 30 MINUTES • SERVES 4

3 medium red capsicums (bell pepper) (600g)

1 teaspoon olive oil

1 large brown onion (200g), sliced thinly

2 cloves garlic, sliced thinly

2 tablespoons brown sugar

2 tablespoons sherry vinegar

3 fresh small red thai (serrano) chillies, seeded, chopped finely

4 x 200g beef eye-fillet steaks

2 corn cobs (800g), trimmed, chopped coarsely

150g (4½ ounces) sugar snap peas

300g (9½ ounces) baby new (chat) potatoes

2 tablespoons coarsely chopped fresh flat-leaf parsley

1 Preheat grill (broiler).

2 Quarter capsicums; discard seeds and membranes. Roast under grill, skin-side up, until skin blisters and blackens. Cover with plastic or paper for 5 minutes, then peel away skin; slice flesh thinly.

3 Heat oil in a medium frying pan over high heat; cook onion and garlic, stirring, for 3 minutes or until soft. Add sugar, vinegar, chilli and capsicum; cook, stirring, for 5 minutes. Season to taste.

4 Cook beef on a heated oiled grill plate (or grill or barbecue) for 4 minutes each side or until browned and cooked as desired. Cover; stand for 5 minutes.

5 Meanwhile, boil, steam or microwave corn, peas and potatoes, separately, until just tender; drain.

6 Top steaks with capsicum relish; serve with vegetables, sprinkle with parsley.

test kitchen notes

Beef rib-eye (scotch fillet) or sirloin (new-york cut) steak can be substituted for the eye-fillet in this recipe. You can make the capsicum relish a day ahead; store, covered, in the refrigerator. Reheat just before serving.

Test Kitchen
NOTE

Za'atar, a blend of
roasted dry herbs,
spices, sesame seeds
and salt, is available
from Middle-Eastern
food shops and some
delicatessens. To make
your own, combine
1 tablespoon each sumac
and sesame seeds with
2 teaspoons finely
chopped fresh thyme
and 1 teaspoon salt.

za'atar-spiced schnitzels with fattoush

PREP + COOK TIME 40 MINUTES • SERVES 4

½ cup (35g) panko (japanese breadcrumbs)

2 tablespoons za'atar

2 teaspoons chopped fresh thyme

8 x 100g (3 ounces) veal scallopine (schnitzel)

⅓ cup (50g) plain (all-purpose) flour

2 eggs, beaten lightly

olive oil, for shallow-frying

FATTOUSH

2 large pitta breads (160g)

250g (8 ounces) cherry tomatoes, halved

2 lebanese cucumbers (260g), cut into ribbons

1 bunch red radishes, sliced thinly

3 green onions (scallions), sliced thinly

1 cup torn fresh flat-leaf parsley

½ cup fresh mint leaves

½ cup (125ml) olive oil

¼ cup (60ml) lemon juice

2 cloves garlic, crushed

1 Make fattoush.

2 Combine breadcrumbs, za'atar and thyme in a shallow bowl. Toss veal in flour, shake off excess. Dip in egg, then press on breadcrumb mixture to coat.

3 Heat oil in a large frying pan oven medium-high heat; cook veal for 2 minutes each side or until golden and cooked through.

4 Serve schnitzels with fattoush.

FATTOUSH Grill bread until crisp; break into small pieces. Combine tomato, cucumber, radish, onion and herbs in a large bowl. Just before serving, toss bread and combined oil, juice and garlic into salad. Season to taste.

We bought uncrumbed (plain) schnitzels to use in this recipe.

Bourbon is a type of American whiskey distilled mainly from corn.

peppered fillet steaks with creamy bourbon sauce

PREP + COOK TIME 20 MINUTES • **SERVES 4**

4 x 125g beef fillet steaks

2 teaspoons cracked black pepper

2 tablespoons olive oil

6 shallots (150g), sliced thinly

1 clove garlic, crushed

⅓ cup (80ml) bourbon

¼ cup (60ml) beef stock

2 teaspoons dijon mustard

300ml pouring cream

1 Rub beef both sides with pepper. Heat half the oil in a large frying pan over medium-high heat; cook beef for 3 minutes each side or until cooked as desired. Remove from pan; cover to keep warm.

2 Heat remaining oil in same pan; cook shallot and garlic, stirring, until shallot softens. Add bourbon; stir until mixture simmers and starts to thicken. Stir in stock, mustard and cream; bring to the boil. Reduce heat; simmer, uncovered, for 5 minutes or until sauce thickens slightly.

3 Serve beef drizzled with sauce.

serving suggestion Fried potatoes and steamed green beans.

test kitchen note

For a medium steak, cook the fillet for about 3 minutes each side; if you like your steak well done, cook a further minute on each side or, for a rarer steak, reduce cooking time to 1 minute each side. Rest the steak, covered loosely with foil, to allow the meat to relax and distribute the juices through the steak.

beef and noodle stir-fry

250g (8 ounces) dried rice stick noodles

2 teaspoons peanut oil

500g (1 pound) beef eye-fillet steaks, sliced thinly

1 tablespoon finely chopped lemon grass, white part only

1 clove garlic, crushed

⅔ cup (160ml) lime juice

⅓ cup (80ml) fish sauce

1 tablespoon coarsely grated palm sugar

100g (3 ounces) chinese mustard leaf, chopped coarsely

1 cup (80g) bean sprouts

½ cup loosely packed fresh coriander leaves (cilantro)

½ cup loosely packed fresh mint leaves

3 green onions (scallions), sliced thinly

1 lebanese cucumber (130g), sliced thinly

1 Place noodles in a large heatproof bowl, cover with boiling water; stand for 5 minutes or until tender, drain.

2 Heat half the oil in a wok; stir-fry beef, in batches, until browned. Remove from wok.

3 Heat remaining oil in wok; stir-fry lemon grass and garlic until fragrant. Return beef to wok with juice, sauce and sugar; stir-fry until heated through. Add noodles; stir-fry until combined. Stir in remaining ingredients; serve immediately.

serving suggestion Sprinkle with thinly sliced red thai (serrano) chilli for an added kick of heat.

test kitchen notes

You can use any Asian greens you like instead of the chinese mustard leaf; try baby tatsoi leaves or chinese water spinach. Baby spinach leaves could also be used. Rice stick noodles, also known as sen lek (Thai) and ho fun (Chinese), are wide, flat noodles made from rice flour.

Fresh rosemary or thyme can be substituted for the oregano.

mustard veal with polenta and spinach puree

PREP + COOK TIME 35 MINUTES · SERVES 4

⅓ cup (95g) wholegrain mustard

2 tablespoons coarsely chopped fresh oregano

4 cloves garlic

8 veal chops (1.5kg)

350g (11 ounces) truss cherry tomatoes

2 cups (500ml) water

1 teaspoon salt

1 cup (170g) polenta

¾ cup (180ml) skim milk

¼ cup (20g) finely grated parmesan

350g (11 ounces) spinach, trimmed

1 anchovy fillet, drained

1 tablespoon lemon juice

1 cup (250ml) beef stock

1 Preheat oven to 180°C/350°F.

2 Meanwhile, place grill shelf on low rung. Preheat grill (broiler) to medium-high heat.

3 Combine mustard, oregano and 2 crushed garlic cloves in a small bowl; brush veal both sides with mixture. Cook veal under grill until browned both sides and cooked as desired.

4 Meanwhile, cook tomatoes on a baking-paper-lined oven tray, in oven, for 10 minutes or until softened.

5 Bring combined water and salt to the boil in a medium saucepan. Stir in polenta, reduce heat to low; cook, stirring, for 10 minutes or until polenta thickens. Stir in milk; cook, stirring, for 5 minutes or until polenta thickens. Stir in parmesan; season to taste.

6 Boil, steam or microwave spinach until just wilted. When cool enough to handle, squeeze out excess liquid with hands. Crush remaining garlic. Blend or process spinach with garlic and remaining ingredients until pureed.

7 Serve veal with tomato, accompany with polenta and spinach mixture; sprinkle with extra oregano leaves before serving, if you like.

serving suggestion Radicchio or rocket salad dressed with balsamic vinegar.

Test Kitchen
NOTE

Polenta is the Italian
answer to mashed
potato – it's the perfect
accompaniment for
soaking up meat juices
and too-good-to-waste
sauces. It is available
in regular and instant
from supermarkets.

fettuccine bolognese

PREP + COOK TIME 30 MINUTES • SERVES 4

2 teaspoons olive oil

1 medium brown onion (150g), chopped finely

2 cloves garlic, crushed

1 medium carrot (120g), chopped finely

1 trimmed celery stalk (100g), chopped finely

500g (1 pound) minced (ground) lean beef

2 cups (500ml) passata

½ cup (125ml) beef stock

375g (12 ounces) fettuccine

1 Heat oil in a large frying pan over high heat; cook onion and garlic, stirring, for 3 minutes or until onion softens. Add carrot and celery to pan; cook, stirring, for 5 minutes or until vegetables are just tender.
2 Add beef; cook, stirring, until beef is changed in colour. Add passata and stock; bring to the boil. Reduce heat; simmer, uncovered, for 15 minutes or until the mixture thickens slightly. Season to taste.
3 Meanwhile, cook pasta in a large saucepan of boiling water until just tender; drain.
4 Serve pasta topped with bolognese sauce.

serving suggestion Green leaf salad and a loaf of crusty ciabatta bread.

test kitchen notes
Passata is sieved tomato puree available from supermarkets. The flavour of the bolognese will improve if it is made a day ahead; reheat just before serving. Substitute beef mince with a combination of pork and veal mince. The mince mixture is suitable to freeze; thaw overnight in the fridge before reheating.

mexican beef wraps

800g (1½ pounds) beef fillet, trimmed, sliced thinly

35g (1¼-ounce) packet taco seasoning

3 cloves garlic, crushed

½ cup (125ml) olive oil

2 large avocados (640g), halved, cut into thin wedges

250g (8 ounces) baby roma tomatoes, quartered

3 green onions (scallions), cut into 5cm (2-inch) lengths, shredded

20 fresh baby coriander sprigs (cilantro)

8 x 20cm (8-inch) flour tortillas, grilled

LIME AND CHILLI MAYONNAISE

1 cup (300g) whole-egg mayonnaise

1½ tablespoons finely grated lime rind

2 tablespoons lime juice

2 tablespoons finely chopped fresh coriander (cilantro)

2 tablespoons finely chopped fresh mint

1½ tablespoons chilli paste

1 Combine beef, seasoning, garlic and half the oil in a large bowl. Cover; refrigerate 3 hours or overnight.
2 Make lime and chilli mayonnaise by combining ingredients in a small bowl; season to taste.
3 Heat remaining oil in a large frying pan over high heat. Cook, beef, in batches, for 6 minutes or until cooked through. Drain on paper towel.
4 Divide mayonnaise mixture, beef, avocado, tomato, onion and coriander sprigs among tortillas. Serve with lemon cheeks, if you like.

test kitchen note
Substitute chicken, lamb or pork for the beef, if preferred.

4 ways with
BEEF BURGERS

classic beef

PREP + COOK TIME 30 MINUTES • **SERVES** 4

Mix 500g (1lb) minced (ground) beef in a bowl with 1 small finely chopped onion, 2 tablespoons finely chopped fresh flat-leaf parsley and 1 clove crushed garlic. Shape into 4 patties; cover, refrigerate for 15 minutes or until firm. Cook patties in a large frying pan over medium heat for 5 minutes each side or until cooked through. Halve and toast 4 bread rolls. Sandwich rolls with a lettuce leaf, pattie, a drizzle of tomato sauce, a slice of tasty cheese and a slice of tomato.

spicy mexican

PREP + COOK TIME 30 MINUTES • **SERVES** 4

Mix 500g (1lb) minced (ground) beef in a bowl with 1 small finely chopped onion, 2 tablespoons finely chopped fresh flat-leaf parsley and 1 clove crushed garlic. Shape into 4 patties; cover, refrigerate for 15 minutes or until firm. Cook patties in a large frying pan over medium heat for 5 minutes each side or until cooked through. Halve and toast 4 bread rolls. Sandwich rolls with 3 thin slices of avocado, pattie, 3 slices jalapeño chilli and 2 tablespoons grated tasty cheese. Drizzle with mild tomato salsa.

antipasto italian

PREP + COOK TIME 30 MINUTES • **SERVES** 4

Mix 500g (1lb) minced (ground) beef in a bowl with
1 small finely chopped onion, 2 tablespoons finely
chopped fresh flat-leaf parsley and 1 clove crushed
garlic. Shape into 4 patties; cover, refrigerate for
15 minutes or until firm. Cook patties in a large
frying pan over medium heat for 5 minutes each side
or until cooked through. Halve and toast 4 bread
rolls. Spread roll bases with sun-dried tomato pesto.
Sandwich rolls with a pattie, 1 slice of char-grilled
eggplant and a quarter of a char-grilled capsicum.
Evenly divide 1 tablespoon each of shaved parmesan
and fresh basil leaves between rolls.

bacon & egg

PREP + COOK TIME 30 MINUTES • **SERVES** 4

Mix 500g (1lb) minced (ground) beef in a bowl with
1 small finely chopped onion, 2 tablespoons finely
chopped fresh flat-leaf parsley and 1 clove crushed
garlic. Shape into 4 patties; cover, refrigerate for
15 minutes or until firm. Cook patties in a large
frying pan over medium heat for 5 minutes each side
or until cooked through. Remove patties from pan;
cover to keep warm. In the same frying pan cook
4 rindless bacon slices until crisp, drain on absorbent
paper. Fry 4 eggs in pan until cooked to your liking.
Halve and toast 4 bread rolls. Spread bases with
barbecue sauce. Sandwich rolls with pattie, 1 rasher
of bacon and an egg.

lamb

stir-fried lamb in black bean sauce

PREP + COOK TIME 30 MINUTES • SERVES 4

⅔ cup (130g) white long-grain rice

600g (1¼ pounds) lamb strips

1 teaspoon chinese five-spice powder

2 teaspoons sesame oil

2 tablespoons peanut oil

2 cloves garlic, crushed

1 teaspoon finely grated fresh ginger

1 medium brown onion (150g), sliced thinly

1 small red capsicum (bell pepper) (150g), sliced thinly

1 small yellow capsicum (bell pepper) (150g), sliced thinly

500g (1 pound) choy sum, chopped coarsely

1 teaspoon cornflour (cornstarch)

½ cup (125ml) chicken stock

1 tablespoon soy sauce

2 tablespoons black bean sauce

6 green onions (scallions), sliced thinly

1 Boil, steam or microwave rice until tender.

2 Meanwhile, place lamb in a medium bowl with spice and sesame oil; toss lamb to coat in mixture.

3 Heat half the peanut oil in a wok over high heat; stir-fry lamb, in batches, until browned lightly. Remove from wok.

4 Heat remaining peanut oil in wok; stir-fry garlic, ginger and brown onion for 3 minutes or until onion just softens. Add capsicum and choy sum to wok; stir-fry for 2 minutes or until capsicum is just tender.

5 Blend cornflour with stock and sauces in a small jug. Return lamb to wok, add cornflour mixture; stir-fry until sauce boils and thickens slightly and lamb is heated through and cooked as desired. Serve stir-fry sprinkled with green onion.

hoisin sweet chilli lamb and vegetable stir-fry

PREP + COOK TIME 15 MINUTES • SERVES 4

100g (3 ounces) dried rice vermicelli noodles

1 tablespoon peanut oil

750g (1½ pounds) lamb strips

400g (12½ ounce) fresh mixed vegetables (see notes)

1 tablespoon finely grated fresh ginger

1 clove garlic, crushed

⅓ cup (80ml) hoisin sauce

2 tablespoons sweet chilli sauce

2 tablespoons water

¼ cup fresh coriander leaves (cilantro)

1 Place noodles in a medium heatproof bowl, cover with boiling water; stand for 5 minutes or until noodles are tender, drain.

2 Heat oil in a wok; stir-fry lamb, in batches, for 3 minutes or until cooked through. Remove lamb from wok.

3 Stir-fry vegetables, ginger and garlic in wok for 5 minutes or until almost tender. Return lamb to wok with noodles, sauces and the water; stir-fry until hot. Season to taste; serve sprinkled with coriander.

test kitchen notes

We used 1 capsicum, 1 bunch pak choy, 1 packet oyster mushrooms and 150g snow peas. Beef, chicken or pork can be substituted for lamb. Recipe is best made just before serving. Use your favourite noodles or rice to replace the rice vermicelli noodles.

tandoori lamb cutlets with tomato and coriander salsa

PREP + COOK TIME 30 MINUTES • SERVES 4

⅔ cup (130g) basmati rice

¼ cup (75g) tandoori paste

¼ cup (70g) greek-style yoghurt

1 tablespoon lemon juice

12 french-trimmed lamb cutlets (600g)

TOMATO AND CORIANDER SALSA

200g (6½-ounce) grape tomatoes, halved

1 small red onion (100g) chopped finely

2 tablespoons fresh micro coriander (cilantro)

1 Boil, steam or microwave rice until tender; drain.

2 Combine paste, yoghurt and juice in a large bowl; add lamb, turn to coat lamb in mixture. Season.

3 Cook lamb on a heated oiled grill plate (or grill or barbecue) for 4 minutes each side or until browned and cooked as desired. Cover; stand for 5 minutes.

4 Make tomato and coriander salsa.

5 Serve lamb with rice and salsa.

tomato and coriander salad Combine ingredients in a small bowl; season to taste.

serving suggestion Accompany with mini pappadums or naan bread and mint raita.

test kitchen note
To get good char-grill marks with no sticking and no mess, line the grill plate with baking paper.

lamb, fetta and spinach parcels

PREP + COOK TIME 40 MINUTES · SERVES 4

600g (1¼ pounds) trimmed spinach

300g (9½ ounces) fetta, crumbled

8 lamb fillets (1.5kg)

16 sheets fillo pastry

cooking-oil spray

250g (8 ounces) rocket (arugula)

½ small red onion (50g), sliced thinly

250g (8 ounces) baby roma (egg) tomatoes, halved

1 lebanese cucumber (130g), sliced thickly

2 tablespoons olive oil

1 tablespoon white balsamic vinegar

lemon wedges, to serve

You could also serve the parcels with a greek salad; see the recipe on page 36.

1 Preheat oven to 240°C/475°F. Oil oven trays; line with baking paper.

2 Boil, steam or microwave spinach until tender; drain. Rinse under cold water; drain well, squeezing to remove any excess liquid. Chop spinach coarsely; combine in a medium bowl with fetta. Season.

3 Cook lamb, in batches, in a heated oiled large frying pan until browned. Cut lamb fillets in half.

4 To make fillo parcels, stack 4 fillo sheets, spraying individual sheets lightly with oil. Cut stack in half widthways; cover with a slightly damp tea towel to prevent drying out. Repeat process with remaining 12 fillo sheets; you will have 8 fillo stacks.

5 Uncover one fillo stack; place on board. Centre two pieces of lamb on stack, top with an eighth of the spinach mixture. Roll stack to enclose filling, fold in sides after first complete turn. Spray parcel with cooking-oil; place on tray. Repeat to make a total of 8 parcels.

6 Bake parcels for 15 minutes or until fillo is browned lightly.

7 Combine rocket, onion, tomato, cucumber, oil and vinegar in a medium bowl; season to taste. Serve parcels with salad; accompany with lemon wedges.

cantonese lamb patties

4 chinese dried mushrooms

1 tablespoon olive oil

1 small brown onion (80g), chopped finely

1 tablespoon finely chopped lemon grass

2 cloves garlic, crushed

1 tablespoon finely grated fresh ginger

1kg (1 pound) minced (ground) lamb

3 green onions (scallions), chopped coarsely

1 tablespoon soy sauce

1 tablespoon hoisin sauce

¼ teaspoon sesame oil

1 egg, beaten

½ cup (35g) breadcrumbs

⅔ cup (130g) jasmine rice

1½ cups (120g) bean sprouts

1 tablespoon fresh mint leaves

SWEET CHILLI LIME DRESSING

¼ cup (60ml) sweet chilli sauce

1 tablespoon water

1 tablespoon lime juice

1 tablespoon finely chopped fresh coriander leaves (cilantro)

1 Cover mushrooms with boiling water in a small heatproof bowl; stand for 20 minutes, drain. Discard stems; chop caps finely.

2 Heat olive oil in a large frying pan over medium-high heat; cook onion, lemon grass, garlic and ginger, stirring, for 4 minutes or until onion is soft. Cool.

3 Combine mushroom and onion mixture in a large bowl with lamb, green onion, sauces, sesame oil, egg and breadcrumbs. Shape mixture into 12 patties; cook, in batches, over medium heat, in a large oiled frying pan until browned and cooked through.

4 Boil, steam or microwave rice until tender; drain.

5 Combine ingredients for sweet chilli lime dressing in a screw-top jar; shake well.

6 Serve patties with rice, sprouts, mint and dressing.

baked lamb chops with capsicum and tomato

PREP + COOK TIME 45 MINUTES · SERVES 4

4 lamb forequarter chops (760g)

2 medium yellow capsicums (bell pepper)
(400g), sliced thickly

375g (12 ounces) cherry truss tomatoes
on the vine

1 small red onion (100g), cut into wedges

2 x 475g (15-ounce) tubs mashed potato

1 Preheat oven to 200°C/400°F.
2 Heat a large flameproof baking dish over high heat.
Cook lamb until browned all over. Add capsicum,
tomato and onion to dish.
3 Transfer dish to oven; roast, uncovered, for
30 minutes or until lamb is cooked through and
vegetables are tender.
4 Microwave mashed potato according to directions
on tub.
5 Serve lamb with vegetables and mashed potato.

serving suggestion Steamed greens (such as peas,
broccolini and beans) sprinkled with 1 tablespoon
of baby mint leaves.

test kitchen note
We used prepared mashed potato, available
from the refrigerated section at supermarkets,
to cut down on cooking time for busy families.
If you're not time poor, make your own
mashed potato to serve with the lamb.

Remove the membranes and seeds from the chilli to lessen the heat.

pesto lamb with zucchini and almond salad

PREP + COOK TIME 25 MINUTES • SERVES 4

⅓ cup (90g) pesto

4 lamb rump steaks (600g)

ZUCCHINI AND ALMOND SALAD

3 medium zucchini (360g), cut into thin ribbons

⅓ cup (45g) blanched almonds, halved, roasted

1 small fresh red thai (serrano) chilli, chopped finely

1 tablespoon lemon juice

2 tablespoons extra virgin olive oil

1 Combine pesto and lamb in a large bowl. Cook lamb on a heated oiled grill plate (or grill or barbecue), for 4 minutes each side or until cooked as desired. Cover with foil; stand for 5 minutes.

2 Make zucchini and almond salad.

3 Serve lamb with salad.

zucchini and almond salad Combine zucchini, nuts and chilli in a large bowl, toss with combined juice and oil until zucchini is well coated. Season to taste.

test kitchen notes

Dress the salad just before serving. The lamb can be marinated in pesto 2 hours ahead or overnight. You can also use lamb cutlets.

lamb and bean nachos with salsa fresca

PREP + COOK TIME 40 MINUTES • SERVES 4-6

1 tablespoon olive oil

500g (1 pound) minced (ground) lamb

1 clove garlic, crushed

1 teaspoon ground cumin

¼ teaspoon chilli powder

400g (12½ ounces) canned crushed tomatoes

425g (13½ ounces) canned Mexe beans, drained

¼ cup (60ml) water

240g (7½ ounces) plain toasted corn chips

1 cup (125g) coarsely grated cheddar

2 medium avocados (500g), mashed

½ cup (120g) sour cream

SALSA FRESCA

4 large roma (egg) tomatoes (360g), chopped finely

1 small red onion (100g), chopped finely

1 tablespoon olive oil

1 tablespoon lemon juice

1 clove garlic, crushed

2 tablespoons finely chopped fresh coriander leaves (cilantro)

1 Preheat oven to 180°C/350°F.

2 Heat oil in a large frying pan over high heat; cook lamb, garlic and spices, stirring, for 5 minutes or until browned. Add tomatoes, beans and the water; bring to the boil. Reduce heat to medium-low; simmer, uncovered, for 10 minutes or until lamb mixture thickens, stirring occasionally.

3 Just before serving, spread corn chips over a large heatproof plate; top with lamb mixture, sprinkle with cheese. Bake nachos, uncovered, for 15 minutes or until heated through.

4 To make salsa fresca, combine ingredients in a medium bowl.

5 Combine avocado with half the salsa in a medium bowl; drop spoonfuls of the avocado mixture and sour cream over nachos. Top with remaining salsa.

tomato and spinach stuffed mini lamb roasts

PREP + COOK TIME 35 MINUTES • **SERVES** 4

½ cup (75g) drained, coarsely chopped sun-dried tomatoes

100g (3 ounces) fetta, crumbled

40g (1½ ounces) baby spinach leaves, chopped coarsely

2 mini lamb roasts (700g)

800g (1½ pounds) kumara (orange sweet potato), cut into wedges

2 tablespoons olive oil

6 sprigs fresh thyme

¼ teaspoon dried chilli flakes

1 Preheat oven to 200°C/400°F.

2 Combine tomato, fetta and spinach in a medium bowl.

3 Cut a horizontal pocket in each roast; do not cut all the way through. Press half the mixture into each pocket; secure with toothpicks.

4 Heat an oiled small ovenproof frying pan over high heat. Cook lamb, turning, until browned all over. Transfer pan to oven; roast lamb, uncovered, for 20 minutes or until cooked as desired. Cover; stand for 10 minutes.

5 Meanwhile, place kumara in a roasting pan, drizzle with oil and sprinkle with thyme and chilli; toss to combine. Season. Roast with lamb for 20 minutes or until golden and tender.

6 Cut lamb into slices; serve with kumara wedges.

Test Kitchen NOTES

Add some chilli to the kumara for extra flavour and heat. The lamb is best stuffed just before roasting; prepare the tomato and spinach filling ahead of time, and store, covered, in the fridge.

lemon and garlic kebabs with greek salad

PREP + COOK TIME 30 MINUTES • **SERVES** 4

8 x 15cm (6-inch) stalks fresh rosemary

800g (1½ pounds) lamb fillets, cut into 3cm (1¼-inch) pieces

3 cloves garlic, crushed

2 tablespoons olive oil

2 teaspoons finely grated lemon rind

1 tablespoon lemon juice

GREEK SALAD

375g (12 ounces) baby roma (egg) tomatoes, halved, cut into wedges

2 lebanese cucumbers (260g), halved lengthways, sliced thinly

1 medium red capsicum (bell pepper) (200g), chopped coarsely

1 medium red onion (170g), sliced thinly

¼ cup (40g) pitted black olives

200g (6½ ounces) fetta, crumbled coarsely

2 teaspoons small fresh oregano leaves

¼ cup (60ml) extra virgin olive oil

2 tablespoons cider vinegar

1 Remove leaves from the bottom two-thirds of each rosemary stalk; sharpen trimmed ends into a point.
2 Thread lamb onto rosemary skewers. Brush kebabs with combined garlic, oil, rind and juice. Cover; refrigerate until required.
3 To make greek salad, combine ingredients in a large bowl; toss gently.
4 Cook kebabs on a heated oiled grill plate (or grill or barbecue) for 10 minutes, turning and brushing with remaining garlic mixture, until cooked.
5 Serve kebabs with greek salad.

Use wooden skewers, if you prefer. If you do so, add 2 teaspoons chopped fresh rosemary to the garlic mixture.

cajun lamb backstraps with four-bean salad

PREP + COOK TIME 25 MINUTES • SERVES 4

1 tablespoon cajun seasoning

800g (1½ pounds) lamb backstraps

1 small red onion (100g), chopped finely

400g (12½ ounces) heirloom cherry tomatoes, halved

60g (2 ounces) baby spinach leaves, shredded finely

600g (1¼ pounds) canned four-bean mix, rinsed, drained

¼ cup firmly packed fresh coriander leaves (cilantro)

¼ cup firmly packed fresh flat-leaf parsley

⅓ cup (80ml) bottled french dressing

lemon wedges, to serve

1 Rub seasoning onto lamb; cook lamb on a heated oiled grill plate (or grill or barbecue) for 4 minutes each side or until browned and cooked as desired. Cover; stand for 5 minutes, then slice lamb thickly.

2 Meanwhile, place remaining ingredients in a large bowl; toss gently to combine.

3 Serve salad topped with lamb; accompany with lemon wedges.

test kitchen note

You can substitute lamb rump or loin chops for the backstraps.

Kipfler potatoes are small, finger-shaped potatoes with a nutty flavour; they're great baked.

lamb rack with herb crust

PREP + COOK TIME 55 MINUTES • SERVES 4

2 cloves garlic, quartered

¼ cup each loosely packed fresh basil, parsley and oregano leaves

¼ cup coarsely chopped fresh chives

1½ tablespoons olive oil

4 x 4 french-trimmed lamb cutlet racks (720g)

500g (1 pound) kipfler (fingerling) potatoes, scrubbed

340g (11 ounces) asparagus, trimmed

1 tablespoon olive oil, extra

lemon wedges, to serve

1 Preheat oven to 200°C/400°F.

2 Process garlic, herbs and oil until smooth.

3 Place lamb in a large shallow baking dish; press herb mixture onto each rack. Roast lamb, uncovered, for 20 minutes or until lamb is cooked as desired. Remove lamb from oven; cover, rest for 10 minutes.

4 Meanwhile, microwave potatoes for 4 minutes. Toss potato and extra oil in a roasting pan, season to taste; roast for 15 minutes. Add asparagus to pan with potatoes and roast for a further 10 minutes or until potatoes are golden and asparagus is tender.

5 Serve lamb with potato and asparagus; accompany with lemon wedges and extra oregano.

test kitchen notes

Substitute your favourite herb combination — for Asian-inspired flavours try coriander and mint. Serve with roasted kumara (orange sweet potato).

lamb with chermoulla and lemon couscous

PREP + COOK TIME 25 MINUTES (+ REFRIGERATION) • SERVES 4

2 tablespoons grated lemon rind

2 cloves garlic, chopped coarsely

2 small fresh red thai (serrano) chillies, chopped coarsely

1 tablespoon finely grated fresh ginger

¼ cup each coarsely chopped fresh flat-leaf parsley and coriander leaves

1 teaspoon sweet paprika

¼ cup (60ml) olive oil

8 trimmed lamb round steaks (1.2kg)

200g (6½ ounces) fresh green and yellow beans

2 tablespoons coarsely chopped fresh coriander leaves (cilantro)

LEMON COUSCOUS

1 small red onion (100g), sliced thinly

1½ cups (300g) pearl couscous

2 cups (500ml) boiling water

40g (1½ ounces) butter

1 tablespoon grated lemon rind

1 tablespoon lemon juice

⅓ cup (25g) unsalted pistachios, chopped coarsely

test kitchen note

The marinated lamb can be frozen for up to 3 months. Defrost in the fridge overnight before cooking.

1 Blend or process rind, garlic, chilli, ginger, herbs, paprika and oil until just combined. Place lamb in a single layer in a shallow dish; coat lamb in mixture. Cover; refrigerate 3 hours or overnight.

2 Cook lamb, in batches, on a heated oiled grill plate (or grill or barbecue) for 4 minutes each side or until cooked as desired. Cover; stand for 5 minutes.

3 To make lemon couscous, cook onion in an oiled frying pan until golden. Add couscous and the boiling water; cover, stand for 10 minutes or until liquid is absorbed, stirring occasionally. Stir in butter, rind, juice and nuts; season to taste.

4 Steam, boil or microwave beans until tender; drain.

5 Serve lamb with lemon couscous and beans; sprinkle with coriander.

4 ways with
LAMB BURRITOS

classic lamb

PREP + COOK TIME 30 MINUTES • **SERVES** 4

Cook 500g (1lb) minced (ground) lamb in a heated oiled pan until browned. Add 35g (1oz) packet Taco Seasoning Mix, 400g (12½oz) canned crushed tomatoes, 425g (13oz) canned Mexe beans and ¼ cup water to pan; boil then reduce heat to medium-low. Simmer, uncovered, for 10 minutes or until mixture thickens; season. Divide mixture between 4 x 20cm (8in) warmed flour tortillas. Divide 1 cup shredded iceberg lettuce, 1 coarsely chopped tomato and ¾ cup grated tasty cheese evenly over lamb mixture, fold to enclose filling.

corn & avocado

PREP + COOK TIME 30 MINUTES • **SERVES** 4

Cook 500g (1lb) minced (ground) lamb in a heated oiled pan until browned. Add 35g (1oz) packet Taco Seasoning Mix, 400g (12½oz) canned crushed tomatoes, 425g (13oz) canned Mexe beans and ¼ cup water to pan; boil then reduce heat to medium-low. Simmer, uncovered, for 10 minutes or until mixture thickens; season. Combine 1 coarsely chopped avocado, 125g (4oz) drained canned corn kernels, 100g (3oz) quartered cherry tomatoes, 1 tablespoon lime juice and 1 tablespoon chopped fresh coriander (cilantro) in a small bowl. Divide lamb mixture between 4 x 20cm (8in) warmed flour tortillas; top with avocado mixture, season. Fold tortilla to enclose filling.

rocket & tomato

PREP + COOK TIME 30 MINUTES • **SERVES** 4

Cook 500g (1lb) minced (ground) lamb in a heated oiled pan until browned. Add 35g (1oz) packet Taco Seasoning Mix, 400g (12½oz) canned crushed tomatoes, 425g (13oz) canned Mexe beans and ¼ cup water to pan; boil then reduce heat to medium-low. Simmer, uncovered, for 10 minutes or until mixture thickens; season. Combine ½ finely chopped small white onion, 150g (4¼oz) quartered yellow cherry tomatoes, 1 clove crushed garlic, 1 finely chopped fresh green chilli and ⅓ cup coarsely chopped fresh coriander (cilantro) in a small bowl. Divide lamb mixture between 4 x 20cm (8in) warmed flour tortillas; top with 50g (1½oz) baby rocket leaves (arugula), tomato mixture and ¾ cup grated tasty cheese. Season to taste. Fold tortilla to enclose filling.

capsicum salsa

PREP + COOK TIME 30 MINUTES • **SERVES** 4

Cook 500g (1lb) minced (ground) lamb in a heated oiled pan until browned. Add 35g (1oz) packet Taco Seasoning Mix, 400g (12½oz) canned crushed tomatoes, 425g (13oz) canned Mexe beans and ¼ cup water to pan; boil then reduce heat to medium-low. Simmer, uncovered, for 10 minutes or until mixture thickens; season. Combine 2 finely chopped, seeded medium tomatoes with 1 large green capsicum (bell pepper), 1 finely chopped, seeded lebanese cucumber, ⅓ cup coarsely chopped fresh mint leaves, 1 clove crushed garlic and 1 tablespoon white balsamic vinegar in a small bowl. Divide lamb mixture between 4 x 20cm (8in) warmed flour tortillas; top with capsicum mixture and 1 cup shredded iceberg lettuce, season. Fold tortilla to enclose filling.

pork

pork and vegetable pancakes

PREP + COOK TIME 25 MINUTES • SERVES 12

12 peking duck pancakes (230g)

1 tablespoon peanut oil

250g (8 ounces) minced (ground) pork

100g (3 ounces) fresh shiitake mushrooms, sliced thinly

1 tablespoon chinese cooking wine (shao hsing)

1 tablespoon japanese soy sauce

1 tablespoon oyster sauce

1 teaspoon sesame oil

1 small carrot (70g), cut into matchsticks

2 small lebanese cucumbers (or 250g qukes), cut into lengths

4 green onions (scallions), sliced thinly

1 To heat pancakes, fold each into quarters then place in a steamer over a large pan of simmering water until warm and pliable.

2 Meanwhile, heat peanut oil in a wok over high heat; stir-fry pork for 4 minutes or until browned. Add mushrooms, stir-fry for 4 minutes or until tender.

3 Add wine, sauces and sesame oil to wok; stir-fry until combined. Season to taste.

4 Serve pork mixture with pancakes, carrot, cucumber and green onion.

Test Kitchen
NOTE

Peking duck pancakes are small pancakes made with plain flour; they are available from Asian food stores and selected supermarkets.

ginger-chilli pork spare ribs

PREP + COOK TIME 1¾ HOURS • SERVES 4

1.5kg (3 pounds) pork spare ribs

6cm (2½-inch) piece fresh ginger (35g), cut into matchsticks

¼ cup (60ml) dry sherry

2 teaspoons sambal oelek

½ cup (125ml) water

1 tablespoon dark soy sauce

1 tablespoon black bean sauce

2 tablespoons caster (superfine) sugar

2 tablespoons honey

1 bunch choy sum (400g)

450g (14½-ounce) packet microwave jasmine rice

1 Place ribs in a large saucepan of boiling water, simmer, uncovered, for 15 minutes; drain, cool.

2 Combine ginger in a small bowl with sherry, sambal, water, sauces, sugar and honey; mix well.

3 Preheat oven to 220°C/425°F. Line a roasting pan with baking paper.

4 Place ribs in pan, add ginger mixture; roast, covered, for 45 minutes. Uncover, roast a further 25 minutes or until ribs are tender and well browned. Remove from pan. Simmer sauce in pan, uncovered, until very thick.

5 Meanwhile, boil, steam or microwave choy sum until just wilted. Microwave rice according to directions on packet.

6 Serve ribs with choy sum and rice; drizzle with warm sauce.

test kitchen notes

Recipe can be made a day ahead; store, covered, in the fridge. You can substitute sambal oelek with 1 fresh long red chilli, finely chopped.

pork and veal
sang choy bau

PREP + COOK TIME 45 MINUTES • SERVES 12

2 tablespoons peanut oil

1 large brown onion (200g), chopped finely

1 large carrot (180g), chopped finely

2 stalks celery (300g), trimmed, chopped finely

2 cloves garlic, crushed

2 teaspoons finely grated fresh ginger

750g (1½ pounds) minced (ground) pork and veal mixture

1 teaspoon sesame oil

¼ cup (60ml) oyster sauce

2 tablespoons sweet chilli sauce

2 tablespoons kecap manis

3 green onions (scallions), sliced thinly

12 butter (boston) lettuces leaves, from the middle of the lettuce

¼ cup (35g) coarsely chopped roasted peanuts

2 tablespoons fresh coriander (cilantro) leaves

1 Heat a wok over medium-high heat. Add peanut oil, onion, carrot, celery, garlic and ginger; stir-fry for 5 minutes or until just softened.

2 Add mince, stir-fry for 5 minutes, breaking up any lumps, or until browned. Stir in sesame oil and sauces for 3 minutes or until syrupy and heated through. Cool for 10 minutes; stir in half the green onion.

3 To serve, spoon mixture into lettuce cups; top with peanuts, remaining green onion and coriander.

test kitchen notes

Add some fresh mint or coriander (cilantro) leaves to the mince mixture. Some butchers and supermarkets sell a pork and veal mince mixture, which is what we used here; if the mixture is not available, buy half the amount in pork mince and half the amount in veal mince.

pork fillet with apple and leek

PREP + COOK TIME 35 MINUTES · SERVES 4

800g (1½ pounds) pork fillets

¾ cup (180ml) chicken stock

2 medium leeks (700g), sliced thickly

1 clove garlic, crushed

2 tablespoons brown sugar

2 tablespoons red wine vinegar

10g (½ ounce) butter

2 medium apples (300g), unpeeled, sliced thinly

1 tablespoon brown sugar, extra

400g (12½ ounces) baby carrots, trimmed

250g (8 ounces) asparagus, trimmed, chopped coarsely

1 Preheat oven to 240°C/475°F.

2 Cook pork in a heated oiled frying pan, over medium-high heat, until browned all over. Place, in a single layer, in a large baking dish; bake, uncovered, for 20 minutes or until pork is cooked as desired. Cover; stand for 5 minutes before slicing thickly.

3 Meanwhile, heat half the stock in a medium frying pan over medium-high heat; cook leek and garlic, stirring, for 10 minutes or until leek softens and browns slightly. Add sugar and vinegar; cook, stirring, for 5 minutes or until leek caramelises.

4 Add remaining stock to pan; bring to the boil. Reduce heat; simmer, uncovered, for 5 minutes or until liquid reduces by half. Place leek mixture in a medium bowl; cover to keep warm.

5 Melt butter in same pan over medium heat; cook apple and extra sugar, stirring, for 5 minutes or until apple is browned and tender.

6 Boil, steam or microwave carrot and asparagus, separately, until just tender; drain.

7 Serve pork with vegetables, caramelised apple and leek; season to taste.

Baby carrots are also sold as 'dutch' carrots. They are available from supermarkets and greengrocers.

Test Kitchen
NOTES

Pork has a natural affinity with both apple and onion; here, these traditional accompaniments are given a contemporary twist. Serve pork with any steamed vegetable that is in season. The leek mixture can be made several hours ahead; store, covered, in the fridge, reheat before serving.

lemon and rosemary pork cutlets

PREP + COOK TIME 35 MINUTES • SERVES 4

2 teaspoons finely grated lemon rind

⅓ cup (80ml) lemon juice

1 tablespoon finely chopped fresh rosemary

2 tablespoons olive oil

4 pork cutlets (940g)

120g (4 ounces) curly endive

⅔ cup (180g) drained char-grilled capsicum (bell pepper)

½ small red onion (50g), sliced thinly

100g (3 ounces) marinated fetta, drained, crumbled

1 Combine rind, juice, rosemary and oil in a small jug, place half the mixture in a medium bowl with pork; turn to coat pork in mixture. Reserve remaining lemon mixture.

2 Cook pork in a heated oiled large frying pan, over medium heat, for 4 minutes each side or until browned and cooked as desired.

3 Combine endive, capsicum, onion and remaining lemon mixture in a large bowl; season to taste. Sprinkle with fetta.

4 Serve pork with salad; sprinkle with extra rosemary leaves, if you like.

test kitchen notes
In the cooler months, serve the cutlets with mashed potato and steamed vegetables.

bbq pork spare ribs with cabbage salad

PREP + COOK TIME 30 MINUTES (+ REFRIGERATION) • SERVES 4

1 cup (250ml) tomato sauce (ketchup)

¼ cup (60ml) worcestershire sauce

½ cup (110g) firmly packed brown sugar

2kg (4 pounds) slabs american-style pork spare ribs

CABBAGE SALAD

¼ medium red cabbage (375g), shredded finely

¼ small green cabbage (300g), shredded finely

2 green onions (scallions), sliced thinly

⅓ cup (45g) toasted unsalted pistachios

½ cup loosely packed fresh flat-leaf parsley leaves

⅓ cup (80ml) honey mustard dressing

1 Combine sauces and sugar in a medium saucepan; bring to the boil. Remove from heat; cool marinade for 10 minutes.

2 Place ribs in a large shallow baking dish, pour marinade all over pork; cover, refrigerate for 3 hours or overnight, turning pork occasionally.

3 Drain ribs; reserve marinade. Cook ribs on a heated oiled grill plate (or grill or barbecue) for 30 minutes or until cooked through, turning and brushing frequently with some reserved marinade.

4 Meanwhile, make cabbage salad.

5 Boil remaining marinade in a small saucepan for 5 minutes or until thickened slightly.

6 Slice ribs into portions; serve with hot marinade and cabbage salad.

CABBAGE SALAD Combine ingredients in a large bowl.

test kitchen notes

Marinated ribs can be frozen for up to 3 months; defrost overnight in the fridge. You could also serve the ribs with char-grilled potatoes, if you prefer.

baked pasta with ham, blue cheese and fennel

PREP + COOK TIME 45 MINUTES • SERVES 4

test kitchen note

Substitute blue cheese for a milder cheese, if you prefer. Ricotta, fetta or cream cheese would work well.

375g (12 ounces) shell pasta

250g (8 ounces) ham, sliced thinly

4 eggs, beaten lightly

300ml pouring cream

½ cup (125ml) milk

200g (6½ ounces) soft blue-vein cheese, crumbled

2 small fennel bulbs (400g), trimmed, sliced thinly, fennel fronds reserved

¼ cup (20g) finely grated parmesan

250g (8 ounces) heirloom cherry tomatoes, halved or quartered

1 tablespoon olive oil

1 Preheat oven to 200°C/400°F.
2 Cook pasta in a large saucepan of boiling water until just tender; drain.
3 Meanwhile, cook ham in a small frying pan, over medium heat, stirring, for 2 minutes or until browned.
4 Combine ham and pasta in a large bowl with egg, cream, milk, cheese and fennel; season. Transfer mixture to an oiled deep 2-litre (8-cup) ovenproof dish; sprinkle with parmesan.
5 Bake, uncovered, for 15 minutes or until pasta is heated through. Toss tomato in oil in a small bowl. Top pasta with tomato mixture; sprinkle with ¼ cup fennel fronds before serving.

serving suggestion Accompany with seeded bread rolls.

pork larb with broccolini and noodles

1 tablespoon peanut oil

2 cloves garlic, crushed

600g (1¼ pounds) minced (ground) pork

⅓ cup (90g) grated palm sugar

2 tablespoons fish sauce

4 fresh kaffir lime leaves, sliced finely

½ cup (40g) fried shallots

⅓ cup (45g) roasted unsalted peanuts

350g (11 ounces) broccolini, trimmed, halved lengthways

250g (8 ounces) fresh egg noodles

1 tablespoon lime juice

1 cup loosely packed fresh coriander leaves (cilantro)

1 fresh long red chilli, sliced thinly

2 tablespoons coarsely chopped roasted unsalted peanuts

1 Heat oil in a wok over high heat; stir-fry garlic and pork for 5 minutes or until pork is browned.

2 Add sugar, sauce, lime leaves, shallots and nuts to wok. Reduce heat to low; stir-fry for 2 minutes or until mixture is slightly dry and sticky.

3 Meanwhile, boil, steam or microwave broccolini; drain well. Cook noodles following packet directions.

4 Remove larb from heat; add juice, three-quarters of the coriander, noodles and broccolini.

5 Serve larb scattered with remaining coriander, chilli and chopped nuts.

test kitchen notes

Substitute broccoli for broccolini. Any leftover larb can be served cold in iceberg lettuce leaves, it makes an easy lunch. Fried shallots are available from Asian grocery stores.

Palm sugar is usually sold in rock-hard cakes that need to be grated. You can use brown sugar if it's not available.

pork, mushroom and sage lasagne

PREP + COOK TIME 2 HOURS • SERVES 6

1 tablespoon olive oil

1 small brown onion (80g), chopped finely

2 cloves garlic, crushed

1 cured chorizo sausage (170g), chopped finely

315g (10 ounces) minced (ground) pork

315g (10 ounces) minced (ground) veal

½ cup (125ml) marsala

½ cup (125ml) chicken stock

6 large sheets dried lasagne (250g)

¾ cup (60g) finely grated parmesan

12 fresh sage leaves, torn

fresh sage leaves, torn, extra, to serve

MUSHROOM MIXTURE

20g (¾ ounce) dried porcini mushrooms

½ cup (125ml) boiling water

15g (½ ounce) butter

1 small brown onion (80g), chopped finely

1 clove garlic, crushed

185g (6 ounces) button mushrooms, sliced thinly

1 tablespoon coarsely shredded fresh sage

WHITE SAUCE

60g (2 ounces) butter

⅓ cup (50g) plain (all-purpose) flour

1.25 litres (5 cups) hot milk

1 Make mushroom mixture and white sauce.

2 Reserve a third of the white sauce; combine remaining sauce with mushroom mixture.

3 Preheat oven to 200°C/400°F.

4 Heat oil in a large frying pan over high heat; cook onion, garlic and chorizo, stirring, for 3 minutes or until onion softens. Add minces to pan; cook, stirring, until browned. Add marsala, stock and reserved porcini liquid; bring to the boil. Reduce heat, simmer, uncovered, for 10 minutes or until liquid is reduced by about a third.

5 Oil a 2-litre (8-cup) ovenproof dish. Place two lasagne sheets in base of dish. Top with half the mince mixture, then half the mushroom mixture; sprinkle with ¼ cup of the parmesan. Repeat layering, finishing with remaining two pasta sheets. Spread with white sauce; top with sage and remaining parmesan.

6 Bake lasagne, uncovered, for 40 minutes or until browned lightly. Stand for 5 minutes before serving.

MUSHROOM MIXTURE Combine porcini with the boiling water in a medium heatproof bowl; stand for 5 minutes. Drain, reserve liquid (for meat mixture); chop porcini finely. Heat butter in a large frying pan over medium heat, add onion and garlic; cook, stirring, for 4 minutes or until onion softens. Add porcini and button mushrooms; cook, stirring, until mushrooms are browned. Add sage; season to taste.

WHITE SAUCE Melt butter in a medium saucepan over high heat, add flour; cook, stirring, until mixture bubbles. Gradually stir in milk; cook, stirring, until mixture boils and thickens. Simmer, stirring, for 2 minutes; season to taste.

pork with ratatouille and potatoes

PREP + COOK TIME 1 HOUR • SERVES 4

1kg (2 pounds) baby new (chat) potatoes, quartered

1 medium brown onion (150g), chopped coarsely

2 cloves garlic, crushed

4 baby eggplants (240g), sliced thickly

6 yellow patty-pan squash (180g), sliced thickly

400g (12½ ounces) canned crushed tomatoes

2 tablespoons finely shredded fresh basil leaves

4 x 150g pork steaks (medallions)

baby sorrel leaves, to serve (optional)

1 Preheat oven to 240°C/475°F.

2 Place potato in a large lightly oiled baking dish; roast, uncovered, for 25 minutes or until potato is browned and crisp.

3 Meanwhile, to make ratatouille, cook onion and garlic in a heated oiled frying pan over high heat, stirring, for 3 minutes or until onion softens. Add eggplant and squash; cook, stirring, for 5 minutes or until vegetables are tender.

4 Stir tomatoes into pan; bring to the boil. Reduce heat; simmer, uncovered, for 5 minutes or until vegetables are tender and sauce thickens. Stir basil into ratatouille; season to taste.

5 Cook pork, in batches, in a heated oiled frying pan over medium-high heat, for 4 minutes each side or until browned and cooked as desired.

6 Serve pork with potatoes and ratatouille; sprinkle with sorrel leaves.

serving suggestion Green leafy salad.

test kitchen notes
Ratatouille can be made a day ahead; store, covered, in the fridge. It is great on its own or served with pasta.

jerk pork cutlets with pumpkin chips

PREP + COOK TIME 45 MINUTES • SERVES 4

3 fresh long green chillies, chopped coarsely

3 green onions (scallions), chopped coarsely

2 cloves garlic, crushed

1 teaspoon ground allspice

1 teaspoon dried thyme

1 teaspoon white (granulated) sugar

1 tablespoon each light soy sauce and lime juice

4 x 280g pork loin chops

1kg (2-pound) piece pumpkin, trimmed

2 tablespoons vegetable oil

PIRI PIRI MAYONNAISE

⅓ cup (100g) mayonnaise

2 tablespoons piri piri sauce

1 Combine chilli, onion, garlic, allspice, thyme, sugar, sauce, juice and pork in a medium bowl.

2 Make piri piri mayonnaise by combining ingredients in a small bowl.

3 Cut pumpkin into 7cm (2¾-inch) chips; boil, steam or microwave until tender. Drain; combine chips with oil in a medium bowl. Cook chips on a heated oiled grill plate (or grill or barbecue) until browned.

4 Meanwhile, cook pork on a heated oiled grill plate (or grill or barbecue) for 4 minutes each side or until cooked through.

5 Serve pork with chips and piri piri mayonnaise.

serving suggestion Green leafy salad.

test kitchen notes

The use of the word 'jerk' in culinary terms refers to a spicy jamaican seasoning used to marinate meat, seafood or poultry before grilling or roasting it. While each cook has their particular favourite combination of spices, jerk almost always contains allspice, thyme and chilli.

pork green curry

test kitchen notes

The meatballs can be made 2 days ahead; store, covered, in the fridge. Curry is suitable to freeze for up to 2 months. Defrost in the fridge overnight before reheating.

800g (1½ pounds) minced (ground) pork

3 teaspoons finely grated fresh ginger

1 fresh long red chilli, chopped finely

2 cloves garlic, crushed

⅓ cup coarsely chopped fresh coriander (cilantro)

1 tablespoon peanut oil

¼ cup (75g) green curry paste

2 x 400ml cans coconut milk

⅔ cup (130g) jasmine rice

2 tablespoons lime juice

1 tablespoon fish sauce

1 tablespoon grated palm sugar

200g (6½ ounces) snake beans, cut into 5cm (2-inch) lengths

⅓ cup loosely packed fresh thai basil leaves

1 Combine pork, ginger, chilli, garlic and half the coriander in a medium bowl; roll level tablespoons of mixture into balls. Heat oil in a large frying pan over high heat; cook meatballs, in batches, for 5 minutes or until browned all over. Remove from pan.

2 Cook curry paste in same pan over medium heat, stirring, for 30 seconds or until fragrant. Add coconut milk; bring to the boil. Reduce heat; simmer, stirring occasionally, for 10 minutes.

3 Boil, steam or microwave rice until tender.

4 Return meatballs to pan with juice, sauce, sugar and beans; simmer, covered, for 5 minutes or until meatballs are cooked through. Remove from heat; stir in basil and remaining coriander. Serve curry with rice.

Chinese barbecued pork is available from Asian butchers and barbecued meat shops.

chinese barbecued pork stir-fry

PREP + COOK TIME 25 MINUTES • SERVES 4

375g (12 ounces) dried rice stick noodles

1 tablespoon sesame oil

1 clove garlic, crushed

1 fresh small red thai (serrano) chilli, seeded, sliced thinly

250g (8 ounces) mixed mushrooms, sliced thickly

175g (1¼ pounds) broccolini, chopped coarsely

2 teaspoons cornflour (cornstarch)

¼ cup (60ml) soy sauce

600g (1¼ pounds) chinese barbecued pork, sliced thickly

1 tablespoon fish sauce

¾ cup (180ml) chicken stock

4 green onions (scallions), sliced thinly

1 Place noodles in a large heatproof bowl, cover with boiling water; stand until just tender, drain.
2 Meanwhile, heat oil in a wok; stir-fry garlic, chilli, mushrooms and broccolini stems for 3 minutes or until mushrooms are just tender.
3 Blend cornflour with the soy sauce in a small jug. Add cornflour mixture to wok with pork, broccolini tops, fish sauce and stock; stir-fry until sauce boils and thickens slightly.
4 Add noodles and onion to wok; stir-fry until mixture is heated through. Serve stir-fry sprinkled with sesame seeds, if you like.

test kitchen note
Use a mixture of your favourite mushrooms in this recipe.

4 ways with
RISOTTO

risotto milanese

PREP + COOK TIME 1 HOUR • **SERVES** 2

Boil 3½ cups chicken stock, ½ cup dry white wine and
¼ teaspoon saffron in a medium saucepan, then simmer,
covered. Heat 25g (¾oz) butter in a large saucepan over
medium heat; cook 1 large finely chopped onion until
soft. Stir 1¾ cups arborio rice into the onion mixture.
Add 1 cup of the stock, stirring over low heat until liquid
is absorbed. Continue adding stock in 1-cup batches,
stirring after each addition, until liquid is absorbed. Total
cooking time should be about 35 minutes or until rice is
tender. Stir in 25g (¾oz) extra butter and 2 tablespoons
each finely grated parmesan and chopped fresh parsley.

hot-smoked salmon & dill

PREP + COOK TIME 1 HOUR • **SERVES** 2

Boil 3½ cups chicken stock, ½ cup dry white wine and
¼ teaspoon saffron in a medium saucepan, then simmer,
covered. Heat 25g (¾oz) butter in a large saucepan over
medium heat; cook 1 large finely chopped onion until soft.
Stir 1¾ cups arborio rice into the onion mixture. Add
1 cup of the stock, stirring over low heat until liquid is
absorbed. Continue adding stock in 1-cup batches, stirring
after each addition, until liquid is absorbed. Total cooking
time should be about 35 minutes or until rice is tender.
Stir in 25g (¾oz) extra butter, 100g (3oz) flaked hot smoked
salmon and 2 tablespoons finely grated parmesan; sprinkle
with 2 tablespoons chopped fresh dill to serve.

prosciutto, peas & chervil

PREP + COOK TIME 1 HOUR • **SERVES** 2

Boil 3½ cups chicken stock, ½ cup dry white wine
and ¼ teaspoon saffron in a medium saucepan, then
simmer, covered. Heat 25g (¾oz) butter in a large
saucepan over medium heat; cook 1 large finely
chopped onion until soft. Stir 1¾ cups arborio rice
into the onion mixture. Add 1 cup of the stock, stirring
over low heat until liquid is absorbed. Continue adding
stock in 1-cup batches, stirring after each addition
until liquid is absorbed. Total cooking time should be
about 35 minutes or until rice is tender. Stir in 25g (¾oz)
extra butter, 4 slices roughly chopped prosciutto, ½ cup
thawed frozen peas and 2 tablespoons finely grated
parmesan, stirring until peas are hot. Sprinkle with
2 tablespoons fresh chervil, to serve.

pumpkin & spinach

PREP + COOK TIME 1 HOUR • **SERVES** 2

Boil, steam or microwave 100g (3oz) chopped
pumpkin. Meanwhile, boil 3½ cups chicken stock,
½ cup dry white wine and ¼ teaspoon saffron in
a medium saucepan, then simmer, covered. Heat
25g (¾oz) butter in a large saucepan over medium
heat; cook 1 large finely chopped onion until soft.
Stir 1¾ cups arborio rice into the onion mixture.
Add 1 cup of the stock, stirring over low heat until
liquid is absorbed. Continue adding stock in 1-cup
batches, stirring after each addition until liquid is
absorbed. Total cooking time should be about
35 minutes or until rice is tender. Stir in 25g (¾oz)
extra butter, pumpkin, 50g (1½oz) baby spinach
leaves and 2 tablespoons finely grated parmesan
until hot. Sprinkle with 2 tablespoons fresh baby
basil leaves to serve.

chicken

apricot chicken with creamy rice

PREP + COOK TIME 1 HOUR • SERVES 4

12 chicken lovely legs (1.2kg) (see note)

2 tablespoons vegetable oil

2 large brown onions (400g), sliced thickly

2 teaspoons finely grated fresh ginger

2 cloves garlic, crushed

3 trimmed celery stalks (300g), chopped finely

425g (13½ ounces) canned apricot nectar

1 cup (250ml) water

40g (1½ ounces) packaged french onion soup mix

1 cup (200g) calrose rice

30g (1 ounce) baby spinach

1 tablespoon finely chopped fresh flat-leaf parsley

1 Remove and discard skin from the chicken if necessary. Heat half the oil in a large frying pan over high heat. Cook chicken, in batches, until browned all over; drain on paper towel.

2 Heat remaining oil in the same pan; cook onion, ginger, garlic and celery, stirring, for 10 minutes or until onion and celery are browned lightly.

3 Return chicken to pan with nectar, the water and soup mix; bring to the boil. Simmer, covered, for 10 minutes. Add rice; simmer, uncovered, stirring occasionally, for 30 minutes or until rice is tender. Stir in spinach. Sprinkle with parsley to serve.

serving suggestion Steamed vegetables or a salad.

chicken saltimbocca

PREP + COOK TIME 45 MINUTES • SERVES 4

test kitchen notes

The word saltimbocca is Italian for 'jumps in the mouth'. The cheese will make the prosciutto stick to the chicken. Remove the toothpicks before serving. This dish goes just as well with a green salad for lunch, as it does with steamed or roasted vegetables for dinner.

150g (4½ ounces) mozzarella

4 chicken breast fillets (800g)

8 slices prosciutto (120g)

16 fresh sage leaves

500g (1 pound) baby new (chat) potatoes, halved

60g (2 ounces) butter

2 tablespoons olive oil

6 fresh sage leaves, extra

⅔ cup (160ml) dry white wine

⅔ cup (160ml) chicken stock

1 tablespoon chopped fresh sage

1 Cut mozzarella into 8 even slices. Cut chicken fillets in half horizontally. Top each chicken piece with a slice of cheese, a slice of prosciutto and 2 sage leaves, securing sage to prosciutto with a toothpicks.
2 Cook potatoes in a saucepan of boiling salted water for 4 minutes to par-boil. Drain.
3 Heat half the butter and half the oil in a large frying pan. Cook extra sage and potato for 2 minutes or until golden. Season; transfer to a bowl to keep warm.
4 Heat remaining oil in same pan over medium heat; cook chicken, sage-side down, in two batches, for 3 minutes each side or until cooked through. Remove from pan; cover to keep warm.
5 Add remaining butter, wine and stock to same pan, bring to the boil; reduce heat, simmer, stirring, for 5 minutes or until liquid reduces slightly. Season.
6 Serve chicken with sauce and potato.

warm pesto chicken with tomato salad

PREP + COOK TIME 30 MINUTES (+ REFRIGERATION) • SERVES 4

500g (1 pound) chicken tenderloins

⅓ cup (90g) sun-dried tomato pesto

¼ (40g) pine nuts, toasted

TOMATO SALAD

100g (3 ounces) baby spinach leaves

600g (1¼ pounds) mixed tomatoes, seeded, chopped coarsely

1 medium red onion (170g), sliced thinly

2 tablespoons lemon juice

2 tablespoons extra virgin olive oil

½ teaspoon cracked black pepper

1 Combine chicken and pesto in a large bowl, cover; refrigerate for 3 hours or overnight.

2 Preheat oven to 200°C/400°F.

3 Place chicken on a wire rack over a baking dish; roast, uncovered, for 25 minutes or until chicken is cooked. Cover; stand for 5 minutes.

4 Meanwhile, to make tomato salad, toss ingredients in a medium bowl; season to taste.

5 Serve chicken with tomato salad; sprinkle with nuts.

test kitchen notes

We used 3 roma tomatoes, 100g grape tomatoes and 250g romatherapy tomatoes in this salad, however, any variety of tomato can be used. The marinated chicken can be frozen for up to 3 months; defrost in the fridge overnight before cooking.

Test Kitchen
NOTE

This recipe can also be made into 'chicken cordon bleu' – chicken filled with ham and cheese. After the fillets have been cut in half horizontally almost all the way through, place a piece of swiss cheese and smoked ham into the opening, secure closed with toothpicks. Continue crumbing the chicken fillets before shallow-frying.

Use prepared mashed potato, available from the refrigerated section at supermarkets, to cut down on cooking time for busy families.

chicken kiev

PREP + COOK TIME 45 MINUTES (+ REFRIGERATION) • SERVES 4

100g (3 ounces) butter, softened

3 cloves garlic, crushed

1 teaspoon finely grated lemon rind

2 tablespoons each finely chopped fresh flat-leaf parsley and chives

4 chicken breast fillets (800g)

⅓ cup (50g) plain (all-purpose) flour

2 eggs, beaten lightly

2 cups (140g) panko (japanese) breadcrumbs

vegetable oil, for deep-frying

600g (1¼-pound) tub mashed potato

340g (11 ounces) asparagus, trimmed

lemon wedges, to serve

1 Combine butter, garlic, rind, parsley and chives in a small bowl; beat with a wooden spoon until combined. Spoon mixture onto a piece of plastic wrap, shape into a 20cm (8-inch) log; wrap tightly, freeze until firm.

2 Cut chicken fillets in half horizontally almost all the way through. Open out fillets, place between sheets of plastic wrap and gently pound with a meat mallet until 1cm (½-inch) thick.

3 Cut butter log into 4 pieces; place a piece of butter at one end of a fillet. Roll once, fold in sides, roll up. Toss chicken roll in flour; dip in egg, then roll in crumbs. Repeat to make a total of 4 rolls. Refrigerate for 30 minutes.

4 Heat oil in a medium saucepan to 160°C/325°F (or until a cube of bread turns golden in 30 seconds). Deep-fry chicken, in two batches, for 10 minutes or until golden and cooked through. Drain well on paper towel.

5 Meanwhile, boil, steam or microwave potato and asparagus, separately, until tender. Serve chicken with vegetables and wedges; season.

Spring onions have small white bulbs; they are sometimes labelled 'globe' or 'salad' onions.

chicken and sugar snap pea pasta

PREP + COOK TIME 25 MINUTES • SERVES 4

test kitchen note
We used tripoline lunghe, a long ribbon-shaped pasta with frilled edges. Any ribbon pasta can be used: fettuccine or pappardelle are fine.

375g (12 ounces) long frill-edged pasta

40g (1½ ounces) butter

1 bunch spring onions (400g), sliced thinly

1 clove garlic, crushed

300g (9½ ounces) sugar snap peas, trimmed

2½ cups (425g) shredded cooked chicken

300ml pouring cream

2 teaspoons wholegrain mustard

2 teaspoons finely grated lemon rind

2 tablespoons lemon juice

50g (1½ ounces) baby spinach

50g (1½ ounces) dry roasted almonds, chopped coarsely

1 Cook pasta in a large saucepan of boiling water until just tender; drain.

2 Meanwhile, melt butter in a medium saucepan over medium heat; cook onion and garlic, stirring, for 4 minutes or until onion is soft. Stir in sugar snap peas and chicken.

3 Stir cream, mustard, rind and juice into pan; cook, stirring, without boiling, for 5 minutes or until thickened slightly.

4 Toss pasta and spinach through sauce; sprinkle with nuts, season to taste.

oven-baked risotto with chicken, rocket and semi-dried tomato

PREP + COOK TIME 45 MINUTES • SERVES 4

1 tablespoon olive oil

1 large brown onion (200g), sliced thinly

2 cloves garlic, crushed

2 cups (400g) arborio rice

¾ cup (180ml) dry white wine

1 litre (4 cups) chicken stock

4 chicken breast fillets (680g)

100g (3 ounces) baby rocket leaves (arugula)

250g (8 ounces) heirloom cherry tomatoes, halved

½ cup (40g) finely grated parmesan

1 tablespoon coarsely chopped fresh flat-leaf parsley

1 Preheat oven to 180°C/350°F.

2 Heat oil in a shallow 3-litre (12-cup) flameproof baking dish over medium-high heat; cook onion and garlic, stirring, for 4 minutes or until onion softens. Add rice; stir to coat in onion mixture. Stir in wine and stock; bring to the boil.

3 Place chicken, in a single layer, on top of the rice mixture; cover. Transfer to oven; bake for 25 minutes or until rice is tender and chicken is cooked through. Remove chicken from pan; stand for 5 minutes.

4 Stir rocket, tomato and a third of the parmesan into risotto. Serve risotto with chicken; sprinkle remaining parmesan and parsley over chicken, season to taste.

serving suggestion Steamed green beans or asparagus.

test kitchen notes

This recipe is best made close to serving. We used a semillon-style wine here, but you can use your favourite dry white wine.

chicken and asparagus ravioli

250g (8 ounces) asparagus, trimmed, halved

200g (6½ ounces) minced (ground) chicken

2 teaspoons olive oil

270g (8½-ounce) packet wonton wrappers

1 egg, beaten lightly

1 medium lemon (140g)

125g (4 ounces) butter

1 clove garlic, crushed

2 tablespoons fresh chervil or small flat-leaf parsley

1 Boil, steam or microwave asparagus until just tender; drain. When cool enough to handle, coarsely chop stalks (don't cut asparagus tops).

2 Combine chicken, oil and asparagus stalks in a medium bowl; season.

3 Brush wonton wrapper with egg. Place 1 rounded teaspoon of chicken mixture in centre of wrapper; top with another wrapper, press edges together to seal. Repeat with remaining wrappers, egg and chicken mixture.

4 Using a vegetable peeler, thinly peel rind from lemon. Cut rind into narrow strips. Squeeze juice from lemon (you need 2 tablespoons of juice).

5 Cook ravioli, in batches, in a large saucepan of boiling water, for 5 minutes or until chicken is cooked through; drain. Divide into bowls.

6 Heat butter in a medium frying pan over medium heat; cook until butter turns a nut-brown colour. Immediately add garlic, then juice; season. Pour sauce over ravioli; sprinkle with chervil. Serve with grated parmesan, if you like.

Chervil, also known as cicely, is a curly leafed herb with a mild fennel flavour.

smoked paprika chicken with tomato and chickpeas

PREP + COOK TIME 1¼ HOURS (+ REFRIGERATION) • SERVES 4

test kitchen notes

Instead of marylands, use chicken cutlets or drumsticks. Marinated chicken can be frozen for up to 3 months; defrost overnight in the fridge.

4 chicken marylands (1.4kg)

1 tablespoon ground turmeric

2 teaspoons smoked paprika

2 teaspoons finely grated lemon rind

1 clove garlic, crushed

⅓ cup (80ml) olive oil

500g (1 pound) cherry truss tomatoes on the vine

400g (12½ ounces) canned chickpeas (garbanzo beans), rinsed, drained

⅓ cup fresh flat-leaf parsley leaves

1 tablespoon lemon juice

1 Using a knife, cut three slashes widthways into each maryland.

2 Combine chicken, turmeric, paprika, rind, garlic and half the oil in a large bowl. Cover; refrigerate for 3 hours or overnight.

3 Preheat oven to 220°C/425°F. Line a roasting pan with baking paper.

4 Place chicken, in a single layer, on a wire rack over a baking dish; roast, uncovered, for 45 minutes or until chicken is tender.

5 Combine tomatoes and half the remaining oil in a small baking dish; roast, uncovered, in oven with the chicken, for 15 minutes or until just tender.

6 Just before serving, add chickpeas, parsley, juice and remaining oil to tomatoes.

serving suggestion Green leaf salad.

chinese barbecued duck salad

1 chinese barbecued duck

200g (6½ ounces) dried rice stick noodles

¾ cup each loosely packed fresh coriander (cilantro) and mint leaves

2 lebanese cucumbers (260g), seeded, sliced thinly

½ cup (75g) toasted cashews

CHILLI LIME DRESSING

1 fresh long green chilli, seeded, chopped finely

1 stalk fresh lemon grass, chopped finely

1 clove garlic, crushed

1 teaspoon coarsely grated lime rind

⅓ cup (80ml) lime juice

2 tablespoons peanut oil

1½ tablespoons brown sugar

1½ tablespoons fish sauce

2 teaspoons sesame oil

1 Remove flesh from duck with skin; chop coarsely. Discard bones.
2 Place noodles in a medium heatproof bowl, cover with boiling water; stand for 5 minutes or until just tender, drain. Rinse under cold water; drain.
3 Make chilli lime dressing by combining ingredients in a screw-top jar; shake well.
4 Combine duck and noodles in a large bowl with herbs and cucumber; drizzle with dressing, toss gently to combine. Top with nuts before serving.

test kitchen notes
You can substitute barbecued chicken for the duck, if you like. Serve with sliced red chilli, thinly sliced green onion and lime wedges.

grilled chicken salad

PREP + COOK TIME 25 MINUTES (+ REFRIGERATION & STANDING) • **SERVES** 4

350g (11 ounces) chicken breast fillets

4 kaffir lime leaves, shredded thinly

1 fresh long red chilli, chopped coarsely

1 tablespoon finely grated fresh ginger

1 clove garlic, crushed

⅓ cup (80ml) lime juice

⅓ cup (80ml) peanut oil

1 lime

2 medium carrots (240g), sliced into long, thin strips (see notes)

2 lebanese cucumbers (260g), cut lengthways into wedges

500g (1 pound) wide fresh rice noodles

350g (11 ounces) gai lan, chopped coarsely

¼ cup firmly packed fresh coriander leaves (cilantro)

LIME DRESSING

¼ cup (60ml) lime juice

¼ cup (70g) sweet chilli sauce

1 teaspoon soy sauce

1 tablespoon caster (superfine) sugar

2 tablespoons peanut oil

2 tablespoons water

2 kaffir lime leaves, sliced thinly

1 Combine chicken, lime leaves, chilli, ginger, garlic, juice and oil in a large bowl, cover; refrigerate for 3 hours or overnight.

2 Cut lime in half, cut each half into three wedges.

3 Drain chicken; discard marinade. Cook chicken on a heated oiled grill plate (or grill or barbecue) for 10 minutes or until browned and cooked through. Cool for 5 minutes. Add lime to grill plate; cook for 2 minutes, turning until browned all over. Cover chicken and lime; refrigerate until cold.

4 Place carrot and cucumber into a bowl of iced water; stand for 30 minutes; drain.

5 Meanwhile, place noodles in a large heatproof bowl, cover with boiling water; separate with a fork, drain.

6 Boil, steam or microwave gai lan until just tender; drain, cool.

7 Make lime dressing by combining ingredients in a screw-top jar; shake well.

8 Just before serving, slice chicken; place in a large bowl with lime wedges, drained carrot and cucumber, noodles, gai lan, coriander and dressing. Toss gently to combine.

Test Kitchen
NOTES

This recipe can be made a day ahead. Cover chicken mixture, vegetables and dressing separately, and refrigerate. Use a julienne peeler to slice the carrot into long thin strips.

chicken and snake bean stir-fry

PREP + COOK TIME 20 MINUTES • SERVES 4

test kitchen notes

In this dish we've used thai basil, also known as bai kaprow or holy basil. If you can't find it, use ordinary sweet basil instead. Snake beans are long, thin green beans that are Asian in origin; if unavailable, you can use green beans.

⅔ cup (130g) jasmine rice

1 tablespoon peanut oil

800g (1½ pounds) chicken thigh fillets, sliced thickly

2 medium white onions (300g), sliced thickly

3 cloves garlic, crushed

1 teaspoon chinese five-spice powder

400g (12½ ounces) snake beans, cut into 5cm (2-inch) lengths

½ cup (125ml) oyster sauce

2 tablespoons light soy sauce

½ cup (75g) cashews, toasted

½ cup loosely packed fresh thai basil leaves

1 fresh long red chilli, sliced thinly diagonally

1 Cook rice according to packet directions until tender; drain.

2 Heat half the oil in a wok over high heat; stir-fry chicken, in batches, until browned all over and cooked through. Remove from wok.

3 Heat remaining oil in wok; stir-fry onion, garlic and five-spice for 3 minutes or until onion softens. Add beans; stir-fry for 4 minutes or until tender.

4 Return chicken to wok with sauces and nuts; stir-fry until sauce boils and thickens slightly.

5 Just before serving, stir in basil. Serve stir-fry with rice; sprinkle with chilli.

serving suggestion Replace the rice with rice noodles, if you prefer.

Serve the stir-fry with steamed jasmine rice or softened rice stick noodles.

honey soy chicken

PREP + COOK TIME 25 MINUTES (+ REFRIGERATION) • **SERVES 4**

¼ cup (90g) honey

¼ cup (60ml) soy sauce

½ teaspoon chinese five-spice powder

1 tablespoon dry sherry

1 clove garlic, crushed

1 teaspoon finely grated fresh ginger

700g (1½ pounds) chicken breast fillets, sliced thinly

1 tablespoon peanut oil

1 large brown onion (200g), sliced thinly

1 tablespoon sesame seeds

500g (1 pound) baby pak choy, quartered

500g (1 pound) choy sum, chopped coarsely

2 tablespoons dry roasted peanuts, coarsely chopped

1 fresh long red chilli, sliced thinly

1 Combine honey, sauce, five-spice, sherry, garlic and ginger in a small screw-top jar; shake well. Place chicken in a medium bowl, combine with half the honey mixture; cover, refrigerate for 3 hours or overnight. Reserve the remaining honey mixture, covered, in the fridge.

2 Drain chicken, discard marinade. Heat half the oil in a wok; stir-fry chicken and onion, in batches, until chicken is browned. Remove from wok.

3 Heat remaining oil in wok; stir-fry seeds until browned lightly. Return chicken to wok with pak choy, choy sum and reserved honey mixture; stir-fry until vegetables are just wilted. Sprinkle with nuts and chilli to serve.

test kitchen note
Baby pak choy is distinguished from baby buk choy by its pale green-coloured stems, while the stems of baby buk choy are white.

mustard rosemary chicken

PREP + COOK TIME 25 MINUTES (+ REFRIGERATION) • SERVES 4

2 tablespoons lemon juice

¼ cup (60ml) olive oil

2 cloves garlic, crushed

2 tablespoons finely chopped fresh rosemary

¼ cup (60g) wholegrain mustard

8 chicken thigh cutlets (1.2kg)

½ cup (125ml) dry white wine

300ml pouring cream

1 teaspoon cornflour (cornstarch)

1 teaspoon water

1 bunch mixed heirloom baby carrots (400g), trimmed, peeled

200g (6½ ounces) baby green beans

1 tablespoon finely chopped fresh rosemary, extra

1 Combine juice, oil, garlic, rosemary, mustard and chicken in a medium bowl, cover; refrigerate for 3 hours or overnight.

2 Drain chicken over a small bowl; reserve marinade. Cook chicken on a heated oiled grill plate (or grill or barbecue) for 10 minutes or until browned all over and cooked through.

3 Meanwhile, place reserved marinade and wine in a small saucepan, bring to the boil; boil for 5 minutes or until reduced by half. Stir in cream, then blended cornflour and the water; bring to the boil, stirring, until mixture thickens slightly.

4 Boil, steam or microwave carrots and beans, separately, until tender.

5 Serve chicken with vegetables; drizzle with sauce and sprinkle with extra rosemary. Accompany with crusty bread, if you like.

Heirloom baby carrots are a colourful mix of purple, orange and yellow baby carrots. They are available from some greengrocers and select supermarkets.

4 ways with PIXXA

ricotta & basil

PREP + COOK TIME 15 MINUTES • **MAKES** 2

Preheat oven to 220°C/425°F. Oil two oven trays or pizza pans. Place 2 large pitta breads or store-bought pizza bases on oven trays; spread with ⅔ cup tomato pasta sauce, top with ½ cup crumbled firm ricotta cheese. Bake for 10 minutes or until bases are crisp. Serve topped with 1 cup loosely packed basil leaves.

chicken & mushroom

PREP + COOK TIME 20 MINUTES • **MAKES** 2

Preheat oven to 220°C/425°F. Oil two oven trays or pizza pans. Place 2 large pitta breads or store-bought pizza bases on oven trays; spread with ⅔ cup tomato pasta sauce, top with 2 cups shredded barbecued chicken, 100g (3oz) halved button mushrooms and ½ cup pizza cheese. Bake for 15 minutes or until bases are crisp. Sprinkle with ⅓ cup loosely packed fresh flat-leaf parsley leaves to serve.

pumpkin & fetta

PREP + COOK TIME 20 MINUTES • **MAKES** 2

Preheat oven to 220°C/425°F. Oil two oven trays or pizza pans. Using a vegetable peeler, slice a 200g (6½oz) piece pumpkin into thin strips. Place 2 large pitta breads or store-bought pizza bases on oven trays; spread with ⅔ cup tomato pasta sauce, then top with pumpkin. Spray with cooking-oil spray; sprinkle with 100g (3oz) crumbled fetta. Bake pizzas for 10 minutes or until pumpkin is tender and bases are crisp. Top with 50g (1½oz) rocket (arugula) to serve.

TIP You can substitute kumara for the pumpkin.

salami & capsicum

PREP + COOK TIME 20 MINUTES • **MAKES** 2

Preheat oven to 220°C/425°F. Oil two oven trays or pizza pans. Place 2 large pitta breads or store-bought pizza bases on oven trays; spread with ⅔ cup tomato pasta sauce, top with 1½ cups coarsely grated mozzarella, 125g (4oz) thinly sliced salami and 85g (3oz) thinly sliced roasted red capsicum. Bake for 15 minutes or until bases are crisp. Sprinkle with ¼ cup loosely packed fresh basil leaves to serve.

seafood

crab cakes with apple salad

PREP + COOK TIME 45 MINUTES (+ REFRIGERATION) • SERVES 6

500g (1 pound) fresh cooked white crab meat

½ cup (150g) whole-egg mayonnaise

1 teaspoon finely grated lemon rind

475g (15-ounce) tub ready-made mashed potato

1 tablespoon each finely chopped fresh chives and fresh flat-leaf parsley

⅓ cup (35g) plain (all-purpose) flour

2 eggs, beaten lightly

1 cup (75g) panko (japanese breadcrumbs)

60g (2 ounces) ghee

APPLE SALAD

2 tablespoons white wine vinegar

⅓ cup (80ml) olive oil

1 teaspoon dijon mustard

3 medium green-skinned apples (450g), cut into matchsticks

1 bunch red radishes, sliced thinly

1½ cups packed fresh coriander leaves (cilantro)

1 Make apple salad.

2 Drain crab meat on paper towel.

3 Stir mayonnaise and rind in a medium bowl; stir in crab, potato and herbs, season. Shape mixture into 12 patties; dust patties in flour, dip in egg, then coat in breadcrumbs. Refrigerate, covered, for 30 minutes.

4 Heat ghee in a large frying pan; cook patties, in batches, until browned lightly both sides, drain.

5 Serve crab cakes with apple salad and lemon wedges, if you like.

APPLE SALAD Whisk vinegar, oil and mustard in a medium bowl until combined. Add apple, radish and coriander; toss gently to combine, season to taste.

pasta primavera with poached salmon

PREP + COOK TIME 40 MINUTES • **SERVES** 4

test kitchen note

You may need a little more liquid in the final pasta dish. Just in case, reserve ½ cup of the pasta cooking liquid and add as required.

- 300g (9½ ounces) fettuccine
- 1.25 litres (5 cups) water
- 2 sprigs fresh dill
- 6 black peppercorns
- 2 teaspoons finely grated lemon rind
- 440g (14 ounces) skinless salmon fillets
- 2 teaspoons olive oil
- 1 medium red onion (170g), sliced thinly
- 2 cloves garlic, crushed
- 170g (5½ ounces) asparagus, halved crossways
- 150g (4½ ounces) snow peas, halved, trimmed
- ½ cup (60g) frozen peas
- 2 tablespoons lemon juice
- 2 teaspoons finely chopped fresh dill
- 2 tablespoons coarsely chopped fresh flat-leaf parsley

1 Cook pasta in a large saucepan of boiling water until tender; drain.

2 Meanwhile, place the water, dill sprigs, peppercorns and half the rind in a large saucepan; add fish. Bring pan to the boil. Reduce heat to medium-low; simmer, uncovered, for 8 minutes, turning fish halfway through poaching time. Remove fish from poaching liquid; discard liquid. When fish is cool enough to handle, flake fish into a medium bowl.

3 Heat oil in same cleaned pan; cook onion, garlic and asparagus, stirring, until asparagus is tender. Add snow peas, peas, juice, remaining rind, pasta and fish to pan; stir until hot (adding a little reserved pasta water if mixture is too thick). Remove from heat; stir in herbs.

fish with mixed vegetables

PREP + COOK TIME 25 MINUTES • **SERVES** 4

⅔ cup (130g) jasmine rice

500g (1 pound) firm white fish fillets, cut into 3cm (1¼-inch) pieces

2 cloves garlic, chopped finely

2½ tablespoons peanut oil

350g (11 ounces) choy sum, chopped coarsely

1 large carrot (180g), cut into matchsticks

150g (4½ ounces) baby corn, halved lengthways

¼ cup (60ml) oyster sauce

1 tablespoon japanese soy sauce

1 tablespoon water

¼ cup fresh coriander (cilantro) leaves

1 Cook rice according to directions on packet until tender.

2 Meanwhile, combine fish, garlic and 2 tablespoons of the oil in a medium bowl.

3 Heat wok; stir-fry fish mixture, in batches, until browned. Remove from wok.

4 Heat remaining oil in wok; stir-fry choy sum stems, carrot and corn until tender. Return fish to wok with choy sum leaves, sauces and the water; stir-fry until hot, season to taste.

5 Sprinkle coriander over stir-fry. Serve with steamed rice and lemon, if you like.

test kitchen note

We used blue-eye (trevally) fillets in this recipe, but you can use any firm white fish fillets.

prawn tamarind stir-fry with buk choy

450g (14½ ounces) hokkien noodles

750g (1½ pounds) uncooked medium king prawns (shrimp)

2 tablespoons peanut oil

4 green onions (scallions), sliced thinly lengthways

4 cloves garlic, sliced thinly

2 teaspoons cornflour (cornstarch)

1 cup (250ml) vegetable stock

⅓ cup (80ml) oyster sauce

2 tablespoons tamarind concentrate (puree)

2 teaspoons sambal oelek

1 tablespoon sesame oil

2 tablespoons lime juice

2 tablespoons brown sugar

200g (6½ ounces) yellow patty-pan squash, sliced thickly

150g (4½ ounces) sugar snap peas, trimmed

500g (1 pound) baby buk choy, chopped coarsely

1 Cook noodles according to packet directions until tender. Cover to keep warm.

2 Meanwhile, shell and devein prawns leaving tails intact.

3 Heat half the peanut oil in a wok over high heat; stir-fry onion and garlic, separately, until browned lightly. Drain on absorbent paper.

4 Blend cornflour and stock in a small jug; stir in sauce, tamarind, sambal, sesame oil, juice and sugar.

5 Heat remaining peanut oil in wok; stir-fry prawns, in batches, for 3 minutes or until just changed in colour and almost cooked through. Remove from wok.

6 Add squash to wok; stir-fry for 4 minutes or until just tender. Add cornflour mixture; stir-fry until sauce boils and thickens slightly. Return prawns to wok with peas and buk choy; stir-fry for 2 minutes or until buk choy just wilts and prawns are cooked through.

7 Serve stir-fry with noodles; top with reserved onion and garlic.

Hokkien are plump, yellow, fresh wheat noodles. A popular stir-fry noodle, they also come in a thin version, which can be used interchangeably with singapore noodles.

Shell the prawns when you get home, and store them in a covered bowl in the fridge. Prawns are best used on the day of purchase, although they will last up to 2 days in the fridge if stored correctly. Uncooked prawns can be frozen for up to 2 months; defrost in the fridge.

tamarind honey prawns with pineapple

PREP + COOK TIME 35 MINUTES • SERVES 4

test kitchen note

Substitute rice or hokkien noodles for the udon noodles, if you prefer.

270g (8½-ounce) packet udon noodles

1.2kg (2½ pounds) uncooked medium king prawns (shrimp)

1 tablespoon vegetable oil

3 cloves garlic, crushed

1 fresh long red chilli, sliced thinly

1 medium red capsicum (bell pepper) (200g), sliced thinly

150g (4½ ounces) snow peas, trimmed

⅓ cup (100g) tamarind concentrate (puree)

2 tablespoons kecap manis

1 tablespoon honey

½ cup (125ml) water

½ small pineapple (450g), chopped coarsely

4 green onions (scallions), sliced thinly

1 tablespoon sesame seeds, toasted

1 Place noodles in a large heatproof bowl, cover with boiling water, separate with a fork; stand for 5 minutes or until tender, drain.

2 Meanwhile, shell and devein prawns, leaving tails intact.

3 Heat oil in a wok; stir-fry prawns, garlic, chilli, capsicum and snow peas until prawns are changed in colour. Add remaining ingredients, except sesame seeds; stir-fry until hot.

4 Serve stir-fry with noodles, sprinkle with seeds.

Tamarind adds a tart, sweet/sour flavour to food. It is available from Asian grocers.

chilli-coconut prawns

⅔ cup (130g) white long-grain rice

750g (1½ pounds) medium uncooked king prawns (shrimp)

1 tablespoon peanut oil

1 large brown onion (200g), sliced thinly

2 cloves garlic, crushed

2 teaspoons finely grated fresh ginger

1 tablespoon each black mustard seeds, ground cumin and ground coriander

2 fresh small red thai (serrano) chillies, chopped finely

8 fresh curry leaves, torn

400ml can coconut cream

½ cup (125ml) water

1 bunch (500g) choy sum, chopped coarsely

2 tablespoons fresh coriander (cilantro) leaves

1 Cook rice according to packet directions until tender. Cover to keep warm.

2 Meanwhile, shell and devein prawns, leaving tails intact.

3 Heat oil in a wok over high heat; stir-fry onion, garlic and ginger for 3 minutes or until onion is soft. Add seeds, cumin, coriander, chilli and curry leaves; cook, stirring, until seeds pop.

4 Add combined coconut cream and the water. Bring to the boil, then simmer, uncovered, for 5 minutes or until sauce thickens. Add prawns and choy sum; simmer, uncovered, for 5 minutes or until prawns change colour and are just cooked.

5 Serve prawns with rice; sprinkle with coriander.

test kitchen notes

To save time, buy shelled prawns with the tails intact from the frozen section of supermarkets; defrost in the fridge before cooking. Serve with steamed asian greens, if you like.

steamed fish and vegetable parcels

PREP + COOK TIME 35 MINUTES • **SERVES** 4

2 medium carrots (240g), cut into matchsticks

2 medium zucchini (240g), cut into matchsticks

4 x 200g (6½ ounces) firm white fish fillets

⅓ cup (80ml) lemon juice

2 tablespoons fresh dill

1 Preheat oven to 200°C/400°F.

2 Divide carrots and zucchini equally between four 30cm (12-inch) squares of baking paper. Top with fish; drizzle with lemon juice. Fold ends and sides of paper over to enclose fish (secure parcel with kitchen string, if necessary).

3 Place parcels on an oven tray; bake for 15 minutes or until fish is just cooked.

4 Serve fish with roasted smashed potatoes, if you like; season to taste. Sprinkle with dill.

test kitchen note
Any firm fish fillets can be used, such as red mullet, murray cod or queenfish.

cajun-spiced fish with roasted corn salad

PREP + COOK TIME 35 MINUTES • SERVES 4

1 clove garlic, crushed

1 tablespoon butter, melted

2 teaspoons sweet paprika

½ teaspoon ground cumin

1 teaspoon ground white pepper

¼ teaspoon cayenne pepper

4 x 200g firm white fish fillets

3 trimmed corn cobs (750g)

1 small red onion (100g), chopped coarsely

1 medium avocado (250g), chopped coarsely

250g (8 ounces) cherry tomatoes, halved

2 tablespoons lime juice

¼ cup coarsely chopped fresh coriander (cilantro)

1 Preheat oven to 200°C/400°F.

2 Combine garlic and butter in a small jug; combine spices in a small bowl.

3 Place fish on an oven tray; brush both sides with garlic mixture, sprinkle with combined spices. Roast, uncovered, for 15 minutes, turning halfway through cooking time, or until browned both sides and cooked as desired.

4 Meanwhile, roast corn on a heated lightly oiled grill plate (or grill or barbecue) for 10 minutes or until browned all over. When corn is just cool enough to handle, cut kernels from cobs with a small, sharp knife.

5 To make salsa, combine corn in a medium bowl with remaining ingredients. Serve fish with salsa and accompany with warmed flour tortillas, if you like.

test kitchen note

We used blue-eye (trevally) fillets in this recipe, but you can use any firm white fish fillets.

char-grilled cuttlefish, rocket and parmesan salad

PREP + COOK TIME 30 MINUTES • SERVES 4

1kg (2 pounds) cuttlefish hoods

2 tablespoons olive oil

1 tablespoon finely grated lemon rind

⅓ cup (80ml) lemon juice

1 clove garlic, crushed

150g (4½ ounces) rocket (arugula)

1 small radicchio (150g), leaves separated

200g (6½ ounces) yellow cherry tomatoes, halved

1 small red onion (100g), sliced thinly

1 tablespoon rinsed, drained baby capers

1 cup (80g) shaved parmesan

2 tablespoons balsamic vinegar

⅓ cup (80ml) olive oil, extra

1 Halve cuttlefish lengthways, score insides in a crosshatch pattern, then cut into 5cm (2-inch) strips. Combine cuttlefish in a medium bowl with oil, rind, juice and garlic, cover; refrigerate for 10 minutes.

2 Meanwhile, combine rocket, radicchio, tomato, onion, capers and parmesan in a large bowl.

3 Drain cuttlefish; discard marinade. Cook cuttlefish, in batches, on a heated oiled grill plate (or grill or barbecue) for 4 minutes or until browned and cooked through.

4 Add cuttlefish to salad with combined vinegar and extra oil; toss gently to combine.

Use your favourite pasta in this recipe. Try penne, conchiglie (a shell-shaped pasta) or other short pasta.

asparagus and salmon pasta

PREP + COOK TIME 25 MINUTES • **SERVES** 4

375g (12 ounces) spiral pasta

340g (11 ounces) asparagus, trimmed, cut into 5cm (2-inch) lengths

415g (13 ounces) canned red salmon, drained, flaked

100g (3 ounces) watercress, trimmed

3 spring onions (75g), sliced thinly

WHOLEGRAIN MUSTARD VINAIGRETTE

1 clove garlic, crushed

2 tablespoons wholegrain mustard

2 tablespoons red wine vinegar

2 tablespoons lemon juice

¼ cup (60ml) olive oil

1 Cook pasta in a large saucepan of boiling water until just tender; drain. Rinse under cold water; drain.
2 Meanwhile, boil, steam or microwave asparagus until just tender; drain. Rinse under cold water; drain.
3 Make wholegrain mustard vinaigrette by combining ingredients in a screw-top jar; shake well.
4 Combine pasta and asparagus in a large bowl with salmon, watercress and onion. Drizzle dressing over pasta; toss gently to combine.

fish fillets with grilled corn salad

PREP + COOK TIME 35 MINUTES • **SERVES** 4

4 x 200g (6½ ounces) murray cod fillets

2 tablespoons soy sauce

GRILLED CORN SALAD

2 corn cobs (500g), silk and husks removed

250g (8 ounces) cherry tomatoes, halved

1 small red onion (100g), sliced thinly

1 fresh small red thai (serrano) chilli, sliced thinly

2 medium avocados (500g), chopped coarsely

¼ cup coarsely chopped fresh coriander (cilantro)

⅓ cup (80ml) lime juice

1 clove garlic, crushed

1 tablespoon olive oil

1 Make grilled corn salad.
2 Brush fish with sauce; cook on a heated lightly oiled grill plate (or grill or barbecue) for 3 minutes each side or until browned and cooked through.
3 Serve fish with salad.

GRILLED CORN SALAD Cook corn on a heated oiled grill plate (or grill or barbecue) until browned and just tender; cool for 10 minutes. Using a sharp knife, remove kernels from cob; combine in a medium bowl with remaining ingredients.

test kitchen note

Before placing in the fridge, remove the fish from the shop packaging; place the fillets on a plate or in a shallow bowl and cover. This will help keep the fish fresher for longer.

Kipfler potatoes are great in salads because they hold their shape well when cooked.

hot-smoked salmon salad

PREP + COOK TIME 30 MINUTES • **SERVES** 4

500g (1 pound) kipfler (fingerling) potatoes

400g (12½ ounces) hot-smoked salmon

100g (3 ounces) snow pea tendrils

1 medium avocado (250g), chopped coarsely

1 lebanese cucumber (130g), halved, sliced thinly

1 small fennel bulb (200g), trimmed, sliced thinly

¼ cup (50g) rinsed, drained baby capers

1 tablespoon dijon mustard

2 teaspoons white (granulated) sugar

2 tablespoons olive oil

1 tablespoon lemon juice

1 Boil, steam or microwave potatoes until just tender; drain. Slice into wedges.

2 Meanwhile, remove any skin and bones from salmon; flake salmon into large pieces. Arrange salmon, potato, tendrils, avocado, cucumber, fennel and capers on a large platter.

3 Combine remaining ingredients in a screw-top jar; shake well, season to taste. Drizzle dressing over salad before serving.

test kitchen note

While most of the smoked salmon we buy has been cold-smoked (cured at a low temperature for a fairly long time), hot-smoked salmon (cured at high temperatures for just a few hours) is generally more moist and not as salty; it doesn't, however, have the same keeping properties as cold-smoked fish.

4 ways with
SEAFOOD KEBABS

lemon & oregano

PREP + COOK TIME 30 MINUTES • **SERVES** 4

Combine 750g (1½lb) uncooked prawns, peeled with tails intact, with 2 teaspoons finely grated lemon rind, 2 tablespoons lemon juice, 1 tablespoon extra virgin olive oil and 1 tablespoon chopped fresh oregano in a large bowl. Thread prawns onto 12 bamboo skewers; season. Preheat oiled grill plate (or grill or barbecue); cook skewers until brown all over and prawns are cooked through. Serve skewers with mixed lettuce leaves and flat bread.

sumac & lemon

PREP + COOK TIME 30 MINUTES • **SERVES** 4

Cut 750g (1½lb) firm white fish fillets into 2.5cm (1in) pieces. Combine fish with 2 teaspoons sumac, 1 tablespoon lemon juice and 1 tablespoon extra virgin olive oil in a large bowl. Thread fish onto 12 bamboo skewers; season. Preheat oiled grill plate (or grill or barbecue); cook skewers until brown all over and fish is cooked through. Serve skewers with rocket leaves.

ginger, soy & coriander

PREP + COOK TIME 30 MINUTES • **SERVES** 4

Combine 750g (1½lb) uncooked prawns, peeled with tails intact, with 2 teaspoons finely grated ginger, 1 tablespoon light soy sauce, 2 teaspoons peanut oil and 1 tablespoon coarsely chopped fresh coriander (cilantro) in a large bowl. Thread prawns onto 12 bamboo skewers; season. Preheat oiled grill plate (or grill or barbecue); cook skewers until brown all over and prawns are cooked through. Serve skewers with a cucumber and chilli salad.

To quickly soak bamboo skewers, place them in a tall jug, fill the jug with boiling water; stand for 5 minutes. You can also use metal skewers, which will speed up the cooking time slightly.

dill, caper & lemon

PREP + COOK TIME 30 MINUTES • **SERVES** 4

Cut 750g (1½lb) ocean trout fillets into 2.5cm (1in) pieces. Combine fish with 1 clove crushed garlic, 2 teaspoons finely grated lemon rind, 2 tablespoons lemon juice, 1 tablespoon extra virgin olive oil, 1 tablespoon rinsed, drain chopped capers and 1 tablespoon chopped fresh dill in a large bowl. Thread fish onto 12 bamboo skewers; season. Preheat oiled grill plate (or grill or barbecue); cook skewers until brown all over and fish is cooked through. Serve skewers with coleslaw.

vegetarian

kumara and coconut curry

PREP + COOK TIME 30 MINUTES • SERVES 4

¼ cup (60ml) olive oil

1 medium leek (350g), white part only, sliced thinly

2 cloves garlic, crushed

⅓ cup (100g) korma paste

300g (9½ ounces) kumara (orange sweet potato), chopped coarsely

270ml canned coconut milk

1 cup (250ml) vegetable stock

400g (12½ ounces) canned diced tomatoes

800g (1½ pounds) canned chickpeas (garbanzo beans), drained, rinsed

400g (12½ ounces) cauliflower, cut into florets

1 tablespoon black mustard seeds

12 fresh curry leaves

200g (6½ ounces) cavolo nero (tuscan cabbage), lightly washed, chopped coarsely

1 Heat 1 tablespoon of the oil in a large saucepan over medium-high heat; cook leek and garlic, stirring, for 2 minutes or until softened.

2 Add paste to pan; cook, stirring, for 2 minutes. Add kumara, coconut milk, stock, tomatoes and chickpeas; bring to the boil. Reduce heat; simmer, covered, for 6 minutes or until kumara is almost tender. Stir in cauliflower, cook for 5 minutes or until tender.

3 Meanwhile, heat remaining oil in a large frying pan over medium heat; cook mustard seeds, stirring, for 1 minute or until seeds pop. Add curry leaves; cook for 1 minute, then stir in cavolo nero (with water still clinging to it). Cook, covered, until cavolo nero is just wilted. Season to taste.

4 Stir cavolo nero into curry mixture to serve.

serving suggestion Naan bread and plain yoghurt.

lentil cottage pie

800g (1½ pounds) medium potatoes, quartered

2 tablespoons butter

1 medium brown onion (150g), chopped finely

1 clove garlic, crushed

400g (12½ ounces) canned crushed tomatoes

1 cup (250ml) vegetable stock

1 cup (250ml) water

2 tablespoons tomato paste

⅓ cup (80ml) dry red wine

⅔ cup (130g) red lentils

1 medium carrot (120g), chopped finely

½ cup (60g) frozen peas, thawed

2 tablespoons worcestershire sauce

⅓ cup coarsely chopped fresh flat-leaf parsley

1 Preheat oven to 220°C/425°F.

2 Boil, steam or microwave potato until tender; drain. Mash in a large bowl with half the butter.

3 Melt remaining butter in a deep medium frying pan over medium heat; cook onion and garlic, stirring, for 4 minutes or until onion softens. Add tomatoes, stock, the water, paste, wine, lentils and carrot to pan; bring to the boil.

4 Reduce heat; simmer, uncovered, for 15 minutes, stirring occasionally. Add peas, sauce and parsley; cook, uncovered, for 5 minutes.

5 Spoon lentil mixture into a shallow 1-litre (4-cup) ovenproof dish. Spread potato mash on top. Bake, uncovered, for 20 minutes. Stand pie for 10 minutes before serving.

serving suggestion Green leafy salad.

Test Kitchen NOTE

If you're not concerned with keeping the fat content of this dish low, you can stir 1 cup of finely grated parmesan into the potato mash before baking the cottage pie.

We used a pinot noir-style red wine here; serve the remaining wine with the meal.

tofu and sugar snap pea stir-fry

PREP + COOK TIME 40 MINUTES (+ STANDING) · SERVES 4

600g (1½ pounds) firm tofu

⅔ cup (130g) white long-grain rice

1 tablespoon sesame oil

1 large red onion (300g), sliced thickly

2 cloves garlic, crushed

2 teaspoons finely grated fresh ginger

1 teaspoon cornflour (cornstarch)

⅓ cup (80ml) soy sauce

200g (6½ ounces) sugar snap peas, trimmed

350g (11 ounces) baby buk choy, chopped lengthways

1 tablespoon brown sugar

⅓ cup (80ml) vegetarian oyster sauce

2 tablespoons mirin

¼ cup fresh coriander leaves (cilantro)

1 Preheat oven to 200°C/400°F.

2 Weight tofu between two boards; stand, tilted, for 10 minutes to remove excess liquid. Cut tofu into 2cm (¾-inch) cubes; pat dry between layers of absorbent paper. Place tofu on baking-paper-lined oven trays. Bake, uncovered, for 10 minutes or until browned lightly.

3 Meanwhile, cook rice according to packet directions until tender.

4 Heat oil in a wok over high heat; stir-fry onion, garlic and ginger for 3 minutes or until onion softens. Add blended cornflour and soy sauce to wok with tofu, peas, buk choy, sugar, oyster sauce and mirin; stir-fry until sauce boils and thickens slightly. Remove from heat, stir in coriander; serve with rice.

test kitchen notes

Buy the smallest baby buk choy you can find. You could also use gai lan or ta gho (available from Asian greengrocers). 'Vegetarian oyster sauce' is made from blended mushrooms and soy sauce. It is available from health-food stores and some supermarkets. Most supermarkets stock mirin. If you can't find it use sweet white wine or sherry, instead.

vegetable, haloumi and rocket salad

PREP + COOK TIME 30 MINUTES • **SERVES** 4

250g (8 ounces) haloumi cheese, cut into 1cm (½-inch) slices

180g (6 ounces) mushrooms, halved (see note)

175g (5½ ounces) vine sweet mini capsicums, halved

3 baby eggplants (180g), chopped coarsely

2 medium zucchini (320g), sliced thickly

½ cup fresh mint leaves

2 tablespoons lemon juice

⅓ cup (95g) greek-style yoghurt

150g (4½ ounce) baby rocket leaves (arugula)

1 Cook haloumi, mushrooms, capsicum, eggplant and zucchini, in batches, on a heated oiled grill plate (or grill or barbecue) until browned lightly and just tender.

2 Meanwhile, process mint, juice and yoghurt until smooth. Season to taste.

3 Combine haloumi and vegetables in a large bowl with rocket; toss gently to combine. Serve drizzled with dressing.

serving suggestion Accompany with toasted wholegrain sourdough bread.

test kitchen note
Haloumi is a sheep-milk cheese that can be grilled or fried, briefly, without breaking down. It should be eaten while still warm as it becomes tough and rubbery on cooling.

A variety of mushrooms, such as portobello, button and swiss browns, will add extra flavour to the dish.

wild mushroom risotto

15g (½ ounce) dried porcini mushrooms

1 litre (4 cups) vegetable stock

2 cups (500ml) water

50g (1½ ounces) butter

100g (3 ounces) chestnut mushrooms, trimmed

100g (3 ounces) button mushrooms, sliced thickly

2 flat mushrooms (160g), halved, sliced thickly

4 shallots (100g), chopped finely

2 cloves garlic, crushed

2 cups (400g) arborio rice

½ cup (125ml) dry white wine

½ cup (40g) finely grated parmesan

2 tablespoons finely chopped fresh parsley

1 Combine porcini mushrooms, stock and the water in a medium saucepan; bring to the boil. Reduce heat; simmer, covered.

2 Meanwhile, melt 30g (1 ounce) of the butter in a large saucepan over medium-high heat; add remaining mushrooms to pan. Cook, stirring, for 5 minutes or until mushrooms are tender and liquid evaporates; remove from pan.

3 Melt remaining butter in same pan; cook shallot and garlic, stirring, for 3 minutes or until shallot softens. Add rice; stir to coat rice in butter mixture. Return mushrooms to pan with wine; bring to the boil. Reduce heat; simmer, uncovered, until liquid has almost evaporated.

4 Add 1 cup of simmering stock mixture to pan; cook, stirring, over low heat, until stock is absorbed. Continue adding stock mixture, in 1-cup batches, stirring, until absorbed between additions. Total cooking time should be about 25 minutes or until rice is tender.

5 Sprinkle risotto with parmesan and parsley to serve. Accompany with crusty bread, if you like.

We used a chardonnay-style white wine here; serve the remaining wine with the meal.

Dried mushrooms are available from delis and some larger supermarkets.

gnocchi with herb and mushroom sauce

PREP + COOK TIME 25 MINUTES • SERVES 4

test kitchen notes

Gnocchi are small dumplings made of ingredients such as flour, potatoes, semolina, ricotta or spinach. You could substitute button or oyster mushrooms for the swiss browns. We used a shiraz-style red wine here; serve the remaining wine with the meal.

1 tablespoon vegetable oil

1 medium brown onion (150g), chopped coarsely

2 cloves garlic, crushed

400g (12½ ounces) swiss brown mushrooms, sliced thinly

1 tablespoon plain (all-purpose) flour

⅓ cup (80ml) dry red wine

1 cup (250ml) vegetable stock

1 tablespoon light sour cream

600g (1¼ pounds) fresh potato gnocchi

¼ cup grated parmesan

2 tablespoons micro herbs, optional

1 Heat oil in a large frying pan over medium heat; cook onion, garlic and mushrooms, stirring, for 5 minutes or until vegetables are just tender. Add flour; cook, stirring, for 1 minute.

2 Add wine, stock and sour cream; cook, stirring, until sauce thickens slightly.

3 Meanwhile, cook gnocchi in a large saucepan of boiling water until gnocchi rise to the surface and are just tender; drain. Add gnocchi to mushroom sauce; toss gently to combine. Sprinkle with parmesan and micro herbs to serve.

serving suggestion Green salad and a loaf of fresh crusty bread.

broad bean and ricotta orecchiette

PREP + COOK TIME 30 MINUTES • SERVES 4

375g (12 ounces) orecchiette pasta

½ cup (125ml) extra virgin olive oil

1 clove garlic, bruised

100g (3 ounces) sourdough bread, torn

2 cups (300g) fresh shelled broad beans (fava beans)

1 clove garlic, extra, crushed

1 teaspoon finely grated lemon rind

¼ cup (60ml) lemon juice

200g (6½ ounces) ricotta, crumbled

½ cup fresh mint leaves

1 Cook pasta in a large saucepan of boiling water until almost tender; drain.

2 Heat 2 tablespoons of the oil in a large frying pan over medium heat. Add bruised garlic and bread; stir for 8 minutes or until bread is golden. Transfer bread to a bowl; discard garlic.

3 Meanwhile, heat 1 tablespoon of the oil in same frying pan over medium heat; cook beans and crushed garlic for 5 minutes or until beans are just tender. Add pasta, rind, juice and remaining oil; stir until pasta is warmed through.

4 Serve pasta topped with pieces of toasted garlic bread, ricotta and mint.

test kitchen notes

Basil can be substituted for mint. If fresh broad beans aren't available use frozen, or substitute with peas. You can also sprinkle the pasta with dried chilli flakes for some extra heat.

felafel wraps

PREP + COOK TIME 45 MINUTES (+ REFRIGERATION) • SERVES 4

¾ cup (110g) frozen broad beans (fava beans), thawed, peeled

400g (12½ ounces) canned chickpeas (garbanzo beans), rinsed, drained

⅓ cup coarsely chopped fresh flat-leaf parsley

1 small red onion (100g), chopped coarsely

⅓ cup (50g) plain (all-purpose) flour

2 teaspoons ground coriander

1 teaspoon ground cumin

1 egg

4 large pitta breads (320g)

1 cup (260g) hummus

50g (1½ ounces) mesclun

125g (4 ounces) cherry tomatoes, halved

MARINATED GRILLED EGGPLANT

6 baby eggplants (360g), sliced thinly lengthways

2 tablespoons olive oil

2 cloves garlic, crushed

1 tablespoon white wine vinegar

2 tablespoons finely chopped fresh flat-leaf parsley

1 Blend or process beans, chickpeas, parsley, onion, flour, spices and egg until almost smooth. Shape rounded tablespoons of mixture into 16 felafel patties. Place on tray, cover; refrigerate for 30 minutes.

2 Meanwhile, make marinated grilled eggplant.

3 Cook felafel on a heated oiled flat plate (or in a frying pan) over medium heat, for 4 minutes each side or until browned and heated through.

4 Spread pittas with hummus; top with mesclun, eggplant, tomato and felafel; roll to enclose filling. Serve with grilled lemons, if you like.

MARINATED GRILLED EGGPLANT Cook eggplant on a heated oiled flat plate (or in a frying pan) over medium heat for 4 minutes or until browned lightly both sides. Combine eggplant in a medium bowl with remaining ingredients.

Test Kitchen
NOTE

To save time when making this recipe, use char-grilled eggplant from the deli.

cauliflower, potato and bean curry

PREP + COOK TIME 30 MINUTES • SERVES 4

4 eggs

1 medium brown onion (150g), sliced thickly

2 fresh small red thai (serrano) chillies, chopped coarsely

1 clove garlic, crushed

2 tablespoons mild curry paste

500g (1 pound) cauliflower florets

4 small potatoes (480g), chopped coarsely

2 cups (500ml) vegetable stock

2 cups (400g) jasmine rice

200g (6½ ounces) green beans, halved

400ml (12½ ounces) light coconut milk

¼ cup loosely packed fresh coriander leaves (cilantro)

1 Boil eggs in a large saucepan of water for 6 minutes or until hard; cool, then peel and halve.
2 Cook onion, chilli and garlic in a heated oiled large saucepan over medium heat, stirring, for 4 minutes or until onion softens. Stir in paste until fragrant. Add cauliflower and potato; cook, stirring, until coated in curry mixture. Add stock, bring to the boil; reduce heat, simmer, covered, for 10 minutes or until potato is just tender.
3 Meanwhile, cook rice according to packet directions until just tender. Cover to keep warm.
4 Stir beans into curry mixture; cook, uncovered, for 3 minutes or until just tender. Stir in coconut milk and egg; simmer, uncovered, until heated through. Serve curry with rice; sprinkle with coriander.

test kitchen note
Accompany the curry with pappadums, and raita made with low-fat yoghurt and cucumber.

roasted capsicum and labne salad

PREP + COOK TIME 30 MINUTES • SERVES 4

2 medium orange capsicums (bell pepper)(400g)

2 medium red capsicums (bell pepper) (400g)

2 medium yellow capsicums (bell pepper) (400g)

2 medium green capsicums (bell pepper) (400g)

80g (2½ ounces) baby rocket leaves (arugula)

1 small red onion (100g), sliced thinly

300g (9½ ounces) labne, drained

2 tablespoons fresh oregano leaves

1 teaspoon za'atar

½ teaspoon chilli flakes

RED WINE VINAIGRETTE

⅓ cup (80ml) olive oil

2 tablespoons red wine vinegar

1 clove garlic, crushed

1 Preheat oven to 200°C/400°F.

2 Quarter capsicums; discard seeds and membranes. Place, skin-side up, on an oven tray. Roast, uncovered, for 20 minutes or until skin blisters and blackens. Cover capsicum with plastic or paper for 5 minutes; peel away skin, then slice capsicum thickly.

3 Make red wine vinaigrette by combining ingredients in a screw-top jar; shake well.

4 Combine capsicum with rocket and onion in a large bowl, add vinaigrette; toss to combine, season. Arrange salad on a large platter, top with labne and oregano; sprinkle with za'atar and chilli.

serving suggestion Accompany with crusty bread.

test kitchen notes
Capsicums can also be grilled (broiled) to remove the skin.

ravioli with pumpkin and sage sauce

PREP + COOK TIME 35 MINUTES • SERVES 4

1 tablespoon olive oil

8 large fresh sage leaves

500g (1 pound) pumpkin, cut into 1cm (½-inch) cubes

4 green onions (scallions), chopped coarsely

1 tablespoon thinly shredded fresh sage

1 tablespoon white balsamic vinegar

625g (1¼ pound) fresh spinach and ricotta ravioli

100g (3 ounces) butter

¾ cup (180ml) vegetable stock

¼ cup (40g) pine nuts

1 Heat oil in a large frying pan over high heat; cook sage leaves, stirring gently, until bright green and crisp. Drain on absorbent paper.

2 Cook pumpkin in same pan, uncovered, stirring occasionally, for 15 minutes or until browned lightly and just tender. Add onion, shredded sage and vinegar; cook, stirring, for 1 minute. Remove from pan; cover to keep warm.

3 Meanwhile, cook ravioli in a large saucepan of boiling water until just tender; drain. Cover to keep warm.

4 Place butter in same cleaned pan; bring to the boil. Reduce heat; simmer, uncovered, for 5 minutes or until nut-brown in colour. Add stock to pan; bring to the boil then reduce heat to low. Return pumpkin mixture to pan with ravioli; stir over low heat until sauce is heated through, season to taste. Top with sage leaves and sprinkle with nuts.

Ravioli, small square pasta pockets stuffed with meat, cheese or vegetables, are sold in the refrigerated section at supermarkets.

antipasto puff pastry tarts.

PREP + COOK TIME 40 MINUTES • SERVES 4

¼ cup (60ml) olive oil

2 cloves garlic, crushed

1 small red capsicum (bell pepper) (150g), chopped coarsely

1 small yellow capsicum (bell pepper) (150g), chopped coarsely

1 medium zucchini (120g), sliced thinly

2 baby eggplants (120g), sliced thinly

1 small red onion (100g), sliced thickly

200g (6½ ounces) grape tomatoes

150g (4½ ounces) baby bocconcini cheese, halved

½ cup (40g) finely grated parmesan

½ cup firmly packed fresh basil leaves

2 sheets ready-rolled puff pastry

⅓ cup (85g) bottled tomato pasta sauce

¼ cup pitted black olives, torn

2 tablespoons baby basil leaves

150g (4½ ounces) mixed salad leaves

1 Preheat oven to 200°C/400°F.

2 Combine oil and garlic in a large bowl. Add capsicum, zucchini, eggplant and onion; toss gently to coat vegetables in mixture, season.

3 Cook vegetables, in batches, on a heated oiled grill plate (or grill or barbecue) until browned lightly and just tender; return to bowl. Add tomato, cheeses and basil; toss gently to combine.

4 Cut pastry sheets in half; fold edges 1cm (½-inch) inward, place on oiled oven trays. Divide sauce among pastry pieces; top with vegetable mixture. Bake for 15 minutes or until pastry has browned lightly.

5 Top tartlets with olives; sprinkle with baby basil leaves and serve with salad leaves.

4 ways with PENNE PASTA

chorizo & tomato

PREP + COOK TIME 15 MINUTES • **SERVES** 4

Cook 375g (12oz) penne pasta in a large saucepan of boiling water until tender; drain. Meanwhile, cook 2 thinly sliced chorizo sausages in a heated oiled large frying pan over high heat until browned. Add 2 cups bottled tomato pasta sauce; bring to the boil. Reduce heat, simmer, uncovered, for 5 minutes or until sauce thickens. Add 100g (3oz) baby spinach leaves and pasta to pan; stir gently until mixture is heated through. Sprinkle with grated parmesan to serve, if you like.

pesto, sun-dried tomato & chicken

PREP + COOK TIME 25 MINUTES • **SERVES** 4

Cook 375g (12oz) penne pasta in a large saucepan of boiling water until tender; drain, reserving ⅓ cup of the cooking liquid. Meanwhile, drain 340g (11oz) semi-dried tomatoes in oil, reserving 2 tablespoons of the oil. Return pasta to pan with ⅓ cup bottled pesto, 2 cups shredded barbecued chicken, tomatoes, reserved oil and cooking liquid. Stir gently until heated through. Sprinkle with grated parmesan to serve, if you like.

tomato & chilli

PREP + COOK TIME 20 MINUTES • **SERVES** 4

Cook 375g (12oz) penne pasta in a large saucepan of boiling water until tender; drain. Meanwhile, heat an oiled large frying pan; cook 1 finely chopped fresh small red thai (serrano) chilli, stirring, for 1 minute or until fragrant. Stir in 3 coarsely chopped medium ripe tomatoes and ¾ cup coarsely chopped fresh flat-leaf parsley; remove from heat. Add sauce mixture to pasta; toss gently. Sprinkle with flaked parmesan to serve, if you like.

This is a great basic pasta sauce; add drained and flaked canned tuna, drained bottled antipasto mix, or slices of salami for quick variations.

creamy mushroom

PREP + COOK TIME 25 MINUTES • **SERVES** 4

Cook 375g (12oz) penne pasta in a large saucepan of boiling water until tender; drain. Cook 300g (9½oz) thinly sliced button mushrooms in a heated oiled large frying pan, stirring, until soft. Add 300ml pouring cream, ½ cup finely grated parmesan and ⅓ cup coarsely chopped fresh chives; stir over low heat until parmesan melts. Add pasta to mushroom mixture; stir until heated through. Accompany with garlic bread, if you like.

GLOSSARY

ALLSPICE also known as pimento or jamaican pepper. Tastes like a blend of cinnamon, clove and nutmeg – all spices.

AMERICAN-STYLE PORK SPARE RIBS usually sold in long slabs or racks of 10 to 12 ribs, trimmed so little fat remains; are the ones to slather with barbecue sauce and cook on the barbie.

BASIL, THAI also known as horapa; is different from sweet basil in both look and taste, having smaller, serrated leaves and purplish stems. It has a slight licorice or aniseed taste.

BEAN
broad also known as fava, windsor and horse beans. Fresh and frozen forms should be peeled twice (discarding both the outer long green pod and the tough beige-green inner shell).
four bean mix a combination of kidney, butter and cannellini beans and chickpeas.
mexe-style beans are a mildly spiced canned combination of kidney or pinto beans, capsicum and tomato.
snake long (about 40cm/16 inches), thin, round, fresh green beans. Asian in origin, with a taste similar to green or french beans, they are mainly used in stir-fries. Are also known as 'yard-long' beans because of their (pre-metric) length.
sprouts also known as bean shoots; tender new growths of assorted beans and seeds germinated for consumption.

BROCCOLINI a cross between broccoli and chinese kale; milder and sweeter than broccoli. Each long stem is topped by a loose floret that closely resembles broccoli; from floret to stem, broccolini is completely edible.

BUK CHOY also known as bok choy, pak choi, chinese white cabbage or chinese chard; has a fresh, mild mustard taste. Use both stems and leaves. Baby buk choy, also known as pak kat farang or shanghai bok choy, is much smaller and more tender than buk choy.

BUTTER use salted butter; 125g is equal to one stick (4 ounces) of butter.

BUTTER (BOSTON) LETTUCE has small, round, loosely formed heads with soft, buttery-textured leaves ranging from pale green on the outer leaves to pale yellow-green on the inner leaves. It has a sweet flavour.

CABBAGE
green, or drumhead, is the most common variety used in recipes. It has a mild fresh taste that deteriorates with over cooking.
red is more densely packed than green cabbage, and has a slightly more bitter taste that starts to deteriorate when cut.

CAPERS the grey-green buds of a warm climate (usually Mediterranean) shrub, sold either dried and salted or pickled in a vinegar brine. Baby capers, those picked early, are very small, fuller-flavoured and more expensive than the full-sized ones. Capers, whether packed in brine or in salt, must be rinsed well before using.

CAYENNE PEPPER a long, thin-fleshed, extremely hot red chilli usually sold dried and ground.

CELERIAC tuberous root with brown skin, white flesh and a celery-like flavour. Can be grated and eaten raw in salads, or boiled and mashed like potatoes.

CHEESE
blue vein mould-treated cheeses mottled with blue veining. Varieties include firm and crumbly stilton types to mild, creamy brie-like cheeses.
haloumi a firm, cream-coloured sheep-milk cheese matured in brine; somewhat like a minty, salty fetta in flavour, haloumi can be grilled or fried, briefly, without breaking down. Should be eaten while still warm as it becomes tough and rubbery on cooling.

CHICKPEAS also called garbanzo beans, hummus or channa; an irregularly round, sandy-coloured legume.

CHILLI available in many types and sizes (generally the smaller the chilli, the hotter it is). Removing membranes and seeds lessens the heat level. Use rubber gloves when seeding and chopping fresh chillies as they can burn your skin.

CHINESE BARBECUED DUCK traditionally cooked in special ovens, this duck has a sweet-sticky coating made from soy sauce, sherry, chinese five-spice powder and hoisin sauce. It is available from Asian food stores.

CHINESE BARBECUED PORK also called char siew. Traditionally cooked in special ovens, its sweet-sticky coating is made from soy sauce, sherry, chinese five-spice powder and hoisin sauce. It is available from Asian food stores.

CHINESE FIVE-SPICE also known as five-spice powder; a fragrant mixture of ground cinnamon, cloves, star anise, sichuan pepper and fennel seeds.

CHORIZO SAUSAGE of Spanish origin, made of coarsely ground pork and highly seasoned with garlic and chilli. They are deeply smoked, dry-cured and very spicy. They are also available raw.

CHOY SUM also known as pakaukeo or flowering cabbage, a member of the buk choy family; easy to identify with its long stems, light green leaves and small yellow flowers. Is eaten, stems and all.

CORIANDER also known as pak chee, cilantro or chinese parsley; bright-green leafy herb with a pungent flavour. Both the stems and roots of coriander are used in Thai cooking; wash well before using. Also available ground or as seeds; these should not be substituted for fresh as the tastes are completely different.

CORNFLOUR also known as cornstarch; used as a thickening agent. Available as 100% maize (corn) and wheaten cornflour.

CREAM we use fresh cream, also known as pouring, pure and single cream, unless otherwise stated. It has no additives unlike commercially thickened cream. Minimum fat content 35%.
sour a thick commercially-cultured soured cream. Minimum fat content 35%.

CURLY ENDIVE also known as frisée, a curly-leafed green vegetable.

CURRY
leaves available fresh or dried and have a mild curry flavour; use like bay leaves. Dried curry leaves keep indefinitely in an airtight container, but their flavour fades over time.
korma paste a classic North-Indian sauce with a rich, yet mild, delicate coconut flavour with hints of garlic, ginger and coriander.
tandoori paste a paste with a medium heat consisting of coriander, tamarind, ginger, garlic, chilli and other spices.

CUTTLEFISH members of a group of molluscs known as cephalopods, which also includes squid and octopus. Has a mild, subtle flavour and a firm texture, which becomes tough if poorly prepared. The flesh is translucent when raw and white when cooked.

EGGPLANT also known as aubergine. Ranging in size from tiny to very large, and in colour from pale-green to deep-purple, eggplant has an equally wide variety of flavours.

FENNEL BULB also known as finocchio or anise; a white to very pale green-white, firm, crisp, roundish vegetable about 8cm-12cm in diameter. The bulb has a slightly sweet, anise flavour but the leaves have a much stronger taste. Is also the name given to dried seeds having a licorice flavour.

FIRM WHITE FISH FILLET blue eye, bream, flathead, swordfish, ling, whiting, jewfish, snapper or sea perch are all good choices. Check for any small pieces of bone in the fillets and use tweezers to remove them.

FLOUR, PLAIN a general all-purpose flour made from wheat.

GAI LAN also known as gai lum, chinese broccoli and chinese kale; is prized more for its stems than coarse leaves.

GARAM MASALA a blend of spices based on cardamom, cinnamon, cloves, coriander, fennel and cumin, roasted and ground together. Black pepper and chilli can be added for a hotter version.

GHEE a type of clarified butter used frequently in Indian cooking; milk solids are cooked until they are a golden brown (whereas in clarified butter they are not), which imparts a nutty flavour and sweet aroma. Ghee can be heated to a high temperature without burning.

KAFFIR LIME LEAVES also known as bai magrood; sold fresh, dried or frozen. Looks like two glossy dark green leaves joined end to end, forming a rounded hourglass shape. Dried leaves are less potent, so double the number called for in a recipe if you substitute them for fresh leaves. A strip of fresh lime peel may be substituted for each kaffir lime leaf.

KECAP MANIS see sauces.

KUMARA the Polynesian name of an orange-fleshed sweet potato tha is often confused with yam.

LABNE a yogurt cheese eaten widely in the Middle East; made by draining yogurt through muslin to remove the liquid. It can be eaten as is, or rolled into balls, coated with herbs and stored in olive oil.

LEBANESE CUCUMBER short, slender and thin-skinned. Probably the most popular variety because of its tender, edible skin, tiny, yielding seeds and sweet, fresh and flavoursome taste.

LEMON GRASS a tall, clumping, lemon-smelling and -tasting, sharp-edged grass; the white lower part of the stem is chopped and used in cooking.

MARSALA a sweet, fortified wine to which additional alcohol has been added, most commonly in the form of brandy. It is available in a range of styles, from sweet to dry.

MESCLUN mixed baby salad leaves also sold as salad mix or gourmet salad mix; a mixture of assorted young lettuce and other green leaves.

MINCE, PORK & VEAL some butchers sell a pork/veal mixture. If this is not available, buy half the amount as pork mince and half the amount as veal mince.

MIRIN a Japanese champagne-coloured cooking wine; made of glutinous rice and alcohol and used expressly for cooking. Should not be confused with sake.

MUSHROOMS
button small, cultivated white mushrooms with a subtle flavour.
chestnut with their small brown caps and long, thin white stems, chestnut mushrooms have a strong, nutty flavour. They also have a low moisture content, so require slightly longer cooking than some other mushrooms. Trim the woody ends from the stems before use. Substitute with swiss browns.
enoki also known as enokitake; grown and bought in clumps, these delicately-flavoured mushrooms have small cream caps on long thin stalks. Available from Asian food shops and most supermarkets.
porcini, dried the richest flavoured mushroom, also known as cèpes. They are expensive but, due to their strong nutty flavour, only small amounts are required for most dishes. Must be rehydrated before use.
shiitake when fresh, are also known as chinese black or forest mushrooms; although cultivated, have the earthiness and taste of wild mushrooms. When dried, they are known as donko or dried Chinese mushrooms; these must be rehydrate before use.

swiss brown also known as cremini or roman, light to dark brown mushrooms with full-bodied flavour. Button or cup mushrooms can be substituted.

MUSTARD SEEDS black, also known as brown mustard seeds, are more pungent than the yellow (or white) seeds used in most prepared mustards.

NOODLES
dried rice stick dried noodles made from rice flour and water, available flat and wide or very thin (vermicelli).
dried rice vermicelli very fine noodles made from rice flour and water. To use, they require soaking in boiling water until they are tender.
fresh egg made from wheat flour and eggs, are sold fresh or dried. They range in width from fine to quite wide. Golden in colour, they only need softening and separating in hot water.
fresh rice also known as ho fun, khao pun, sen yau, pho or kway tiau, depending on the country of manufacture. Can be purchased in strands of various widths or large sheets weighing about 500g, which are cut into the noodle size desired. Chewy and pure white, they do not need pre-cooking before use.
hokkien also known as stir-fry noodles; fresh wheat noodles resembling thick, yellow-brown spaghetti needing no pre-cooking before being used.
udon available fresh and dried, these broad, white Japanese wheat noodles, are often found hot in soup, although they may also be served cold.

ORECCHIETTE small disc-shaped pasta, translates literally as 'little ears'.

PAK CHOY similar to baby buk choy, except the stem is a very pale green, rather than white, and the top is less leafy.

PANKO also known as Japanese breadcrumbs; are available from Asian grocery stores and many supermarkets. If you can't find the Japanese variety, use stale breadcrumbs, instead.

PASSATA sieved tomato puree available from supermarkets.

PATTY-PAN SQUASH also known as crookneck or custard marrow pumpkins; a round, slightly flat summer squash being yellow to pale-green in colour and having a scalloped edge. It has a firm white flesh and a distinct flavour.

PEKING DUCK PANCAKES small, round crepes or pancakes made with plain flour; available from Asian food stores. To prepare, place in a steamer set over a large pan of simmering water. Steam for 5 minutes or until warm and pliable.

POLENTA a coarsely ground yellow cornmeal used for making cornmeal muffins and cornbread; it gives cakes a particularly dense texture. It is also the name of the dish made from it.

POTATOES
baby baby new potatoes also known as chats; not a separate variety but an early harvest with very thin skin.
kipfler small, finger-shaped, knobby potato with a nutty flavour; great baked and in salads as it holds its shape well when cooked.

PROSCIUTTO a thinly-sliced, dry-cured ham originating in Italy; comes in two varieties: prosciutto crudo (raw) and prosciutto cotto (cooked).

QUKES baby Lebanese cucumbers.

RED RADISH a peppery root vegetable related to the mustard plant. The small round red variety is the mildest.

RICE
arborio a small, round-grain rice that is well-suited to absorb a large amount of liquid; especially suitable for risottos.
basmati a white, fragrant long-grain rice. Wash several times before cooking.
calrose a medium-grain rice that is extremely versatile; can substitute for short- or long-grain rice if necessary.
jasmine fragrant long-grain rice; white rice can be substituted, but will not taste the same.

ROCKET also known as arugula, rugula and rucola; a peppery-tasting green leaf that can be used similarly to baby spinach leaves, eaten raw in salad or cooked.

SAMBAL OELEK (also ulek or olek) Indonesian in origin; a salty paste made from ground chillies and vinegar. It is used to add heat to dishes without altering the other flavours.

SAUCES
black bean a Chinese sauce made from fermented soya beans, spices and flour.
fish made from pulverised salted fermented fish, most often anchovies. Has a pungent smell and strong taste, so use sparingly.

oyster Asian in origin, this rich, brown sauce is made from oysters and their brine, cooked with salt and soy sauce, and thickened with starches.
vegetarian oyster is made from blended mushrooms and soy sauce.
piri piri an extremely hot tasting sauce from West Africa made using dried piri piri chillies.
soy made from fermented soya beans. Several variations are available in most supermarkets and Asian food stores.
dark soy deep brown, almost black in colour; is rich with a thicker consistency than other types. Pungent but not salty, it is good for marinating.
japanese soy an all-purpose low-sodium soy sauce made with more wheat content than its Chinese counterparts; fermented in barrels and aged. Possibly the best table soy and the one to choose if you only want one variety.
kecap manis a dark, thick sweet soy sauce used in most South-East Asian cuisines. The soy's sweetness is derived from the addition of either molasses or palm sugar when brewed.
light soy fairly thin in consistency and, while paler than the others, the saltiest tasting; used in dishes in which the natural colour of the ingredients is to be maintained. Not to be confused with salt-reduced or low-sodium soy sauces.
sweet chilli a mild sauce made from red chillies, sugar, garlic and vinegar.
tomato also known as ketchup or catsup; a flavoured condiment made using tomatoes, vinegar and spices.
worcestershire a dark coloured sauce made from garlic, soy sauce, tamarind, onions, molasses, lime, anchovies, vinegar and other seasonings.

SNOW PEA SPROUTS the tender new growths of snow peas; also known as mange tout (eat all).

SPINACH also known as english spinach and incorrectly, silver beet. Its thick, soft oval leaves and green stems are both edible. Baby spinach is also available.

SUGAR
brown a very soft, finely granulated sugar retaining molasses for its characteristic colour and flavour.
caster also known as superfine or finely granulated table sugar.

palm also known as nam tan pip, jaggery, jawa or gula melaka; made from the sap of the sugar palm tree. Light brown to black in colour and usually sold in rock-hard cakes. Substitute with brown sugar if unavailable.
white a coarsely granulated sugar, also known as table or crystal sugar.

SUGAR SNAP PEAS also known as honey snap peas; fresh small peas that can be eaten whole, pod and all, similarly to snow peas.

TAMARIND PUREE (or concentrate or paste) the distillation of tamarind juice into a condensed, compacted paste. Thick and purple-black, it requires no soaking or straining.

TUSCAN CABBAGE (also known as cavolo nero or tuscan black cabbage) it has long, narrow, wrinkled leaves and a rich and astringent, mild cabbage flavour. It doesn't lose its volume like silver beet or spinach when cooked, but it does need longer cooking. If you can't find it, use cabbage or silver beet instead.

VINEGAR
balsamic made from the juice of the Trebbiano grape; has a deep rich brown colour with a sweet and sour flavour.
white balsamic vinegar (condiment) is a clear and lighter version of balsamic vinegar; it has a fresh, sweet clean taste.
cider (apple cider) made from crushed fermented apples.
red wine based on fermented red wine.
rice a colourless vinegar made from fermented rice and flavoured with sugar and salt. It is also known as seasoned rice vinegar.
sherry made from a blend of wines and left in wooden vats to mature where they develop a rich mellow flavour.
white made from spirit of cane sugar.

WONTON WRAPPERS also known as wonton skins; made of flour, eggs and water, they come in varying thicknesses. Sold packaged in large amounts and found in the refrigerated section of Asian grocery stores; gow gee, egg or spring roll pastry sheets can be substituted.

ZA'ATAR a blend of roasted sesame seeds, sumac and dried herbs such as thyme and oregano; its content is largely determined by the maker. Available from specialist and Middle Eastern food stores.

INDEX

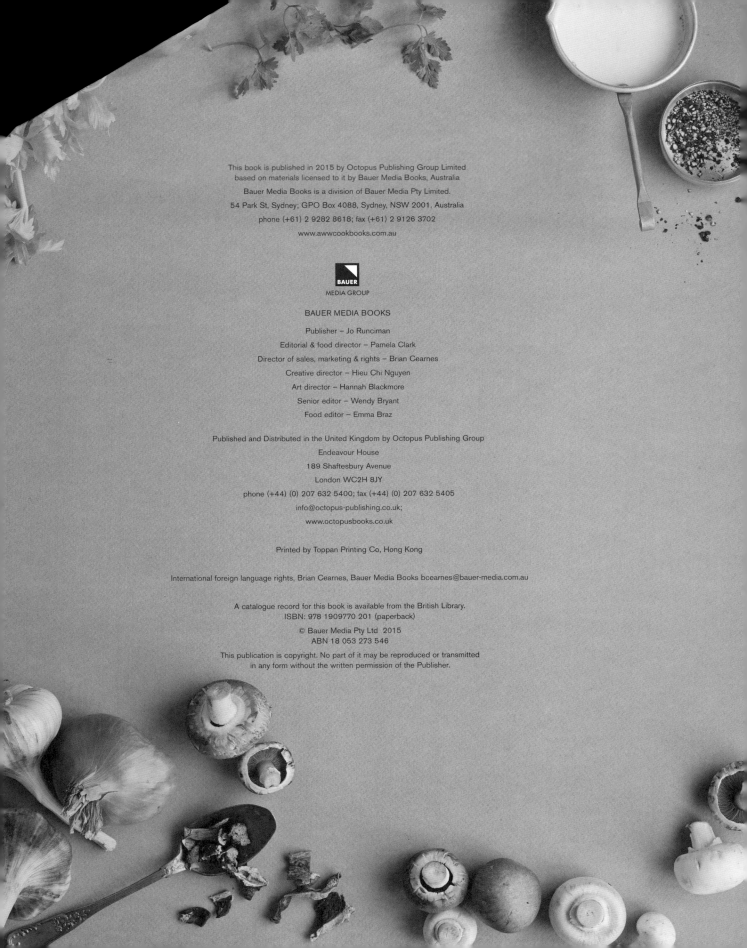

This book is published in 2015 by Octopus Publishing Group Limited
based on materials licensed to it by Bauer Media Books, Australia

Bauer Media Books is a division of Bauer Media Pty Limited.

54 Park St, Sydney; GPO Box 4088, Sydney, NSW 2001, Australia

phone (+61) 2 9282 8618; fax (+61) 2 9126 3702

www.awwcookbooks.com.au

BAUER

MEDIA GROUP

BAUER MEDIA BOOKS

Publisher – Jo Runciman

Editorial & food director – Pamela Clark

Director of sales, marketing & rights – Brian Cearnes

Creative director – Hieu Chi Nguyen

Art director – Hannah Blackmore

Senior editor – Wendy Bryant

Food editor – Emma Braz

Published and Distributed in the United Kingdom by Octopus Publishing Group

Endeavour House

189 Shaftesbury Avenue

London WC2H 8JY

phone (+44) (0) 207 632 5400; fax (+44) (0) 207 632 5405

info@octopus-publishing.co.uk;

www.octopusbooks.co.uk

Printed by Toppan Printing Co, Hong Kong

International foreign language rights, Brian Cearnes, Bauer Media Books bcearnes@bauer-media.com.au

A catalogue record for this book is available from the British Library.
ISBN: 978 1909770 201 (paperback)

© Bauer Media Pty Ltd 2015
ABN 18 053 273 546

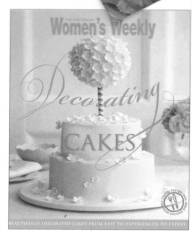

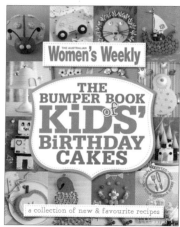